Fiscal Policy Convergenc
Reagan to Blair

Ideas drove the convergence of American and British and conservative and New Left approaches to a restrained fiscal policy in the era of neo-liberalism. Ravi Roy's and Arthur Denzau's compelling, elegant, and concise argument makes us think about the likely course of divergence in policy approaches in an era of unrestrained fiscal policy and counter-terrorist warfare. This book speaks to core concerns of specialists, and will be a source of intellectual pleasure for the interested general reader.

Peter J. Katzenstein *Walter S. Carpenter, Jr. Professor of International Studies, Cornell University*

It is often assumed that left-of-center governments in the US and Britain support policies that would lead to ever-increasing public spending and higher taxes. Right-of-center governments, by way of contrast, are expected to support policies that reduce public spending and lower taxes. These characterizations were reinforced with the advent of Reaganomics and Thatcherite economic policy in the 1980s.

The elections of Bill Clinton and Tony Blair in the 1990s paradoxically saw the consolidation and completion of critical aspects of the Reagan–Thatcher fiscal agenda, a process that *Fiscal Policy Convergence from Reagan to Blair* critically analyzes. It has previously been thought that the process of adopting common fiscal policies was caused by economic integration and globalization, but this book reveals a much more comprehensive explanation—and one that includes domestic factors.

Whether fiscal policy conversion is seen as a good or bad occurrence, this book will unite both left and right to better explain the process. Students and academics of international political economy, public policy and politics will find this book a good addition to their reading lists.

Ravi K. Roy is Visiting Research Fellow at the Claremont Institute for Economic Policy Studies, USA.

Arthur T. Denzau is Economics Department Chair and Dean of the School of Politics and Economics at the Claremont Graduate University, USA.

Routledge Frontiers of Political Economy

Fiscal Policy Convergence from Reagan to Blair

The left veers right

Ravi K. Roy and Arthur T. Denzau

Routledge
Taylor & Francis Group

LONDON AND NEW YORK

First published 2004
by Routledge

2 Park Square, Milton Park, Abingdon, Oxfordshire OX14 4RN

Simultaneously published in the USA and Canada
by Routledge

711 Third Avenue, New York, NY 10017

First issued in paperback 2014

Routledge is an imprint of the Taylor & Francis Group, an informa company

© 2004 Ravi K. Roy and Arthur T. Denzau

Typeset in Sabon by
HWA Text and Data Management, Tunbridge Wells

British Library Cataloguing in Publication Data
A catalogue record for this book is available from the British Library

Library of Congress Cataloging in Publication Data
A catalog record for this book has been requested

ISBN 978-0-415-32413-7 (hbk)

ISBN 978-0-415-75870-3 (pbk)

This book is dedicated to the Lord God and to the memory of my sweet mother Letta Argus Roy.

Contents

Illustrations

Foreword

This book can be read at two levels. One is as a fascinating account of a set of high-profile economic policy episodes, the fiscal policy battles of the Reagan, Thatcher, Clinton, and Blair administrations. The second is as an important contribution to the literature on the role of ideas in economic policy making. A number of scholars have viewed the espousal of particular economic theories or ideologies in the public arena as merely rationalizations for the pursuit of particular interests. However, as Roy and Denzau make clear, that is far too simple a characterization. There is certainly reason to be cynical about whether interested parties always believe the public arguments that they make, but we cannot formulate our interests without at least implicit ideas about our objectives and how the world works.

Ideas about how economies work have undergone some important changes in recent decades. There is now a rather broad consensus that although a little inflation may be good for growth in the short run, it is bad in the long run. Likewise, the disappointing results of market liberalization in Russia have helped to focus greater attention on the prerequisites for well-functioning markets, such as clear property rights, a legitimate legal system, and political stability.

Equally important have been changing beliefs about fiscal policy. Although perhaps most famous or "infamous" were the supply-side tax cuts of the Reagan administration, Roy and Denzau convincingly argue that the neoliberal revolution in fiscal policy was much broader than the simple (and often false) idea that tax cuts will pay for themselves. A cynic can interpret the simple supply-side view as an attempt to form a coalition based on the pie-in-the-sky belief that good conservative objectives—both to cut taxes and balance the budget while increasing military spending—need not conflict. The authors, however, convincingly show that there was more to Reaganomics than this. They provide a broader interpretation of the neoliberal paradigm that was embraced by Reagan and Thatcher and, more surprisingly, by Clinton and Blair.

Stressing the interplay of ideas, coalitions, and institutions in fashioning major shifts in economic policy, the authors argue that Reagan and Thatcher sought systematically to reconcentrate power in the highest levels of the executive for the purpose of dismantling the redistributive Keynesian welfare state policy apparatus. Stagflation and poor economic growth in the 1970s, combined with the rapid rise of international markets, caused politicians, constituents, policy bureaucrats, and academic advisors to rethink traditional policy beliefs and to propel new policy trajectories. The authors explain how a shift from Keynesian ideas toward neoliberalism influenced the fiscal policy strategies of New Democrats and New Labour in both the White House and Whitehall. We have found that while Reagan, Thatcher, Clinton, and Blair all adopted broadly similar neoliberal beliefs, each achieved discrete results in instituting them. The authors also distinguish between distinct core beliefs and secondary policy beliefs that exist within the neoliberal paradigm itself. They argue effectively that although all four leaders may be termed *neoliberals* in the broad sense, each followed a distinct neoliberal fiscal course that entailed distinct fiscal policy priorities. In making this distinction, the authors provide an engaging account of the fiscal convergence in the United States and Britain.

This book is highly recommended not only to students of the role of ideas in policy making but to anyone interested in the fascinating history of fiscal policy change in Britain and the United States.

Thomas D. Willett

Preface

In the wake of the Great Depression of the 1930s, which became associated with the failings of traditional laissez-faire capitalism in the United States and Britain, the Democratic and Labour parties in the post-World War II era followed a new economic paradigm that supported increased government intervention and management over their economies. This paradigm was based on the ideas and theories of the English economist John Maynard Keynes, who proposed in his seminal work, *The General Theory of Employment, Interest and Money* (1936), that the economy moves in cycles under certain conditions in very specific ways. *Keynesianism*, as it would become known, challenged the traditional neoclassical assumption that there existed in capitalist economies a natural tendency of the market mechanism to self-correct for economic shocks and to maintain an equilibrium at full employment.

Keynes believed that aggregate output—and consequently employment—was a function of aggregate demand. Accordingly, Keynes attributed rises in unemployment to a shortage of private capital investment and spending in the economy. For this shortfall, he blamed short-sighted private investors, whose investment decisions were often guided by irrational expectations and fears about future profitability. Negative expectations, he asserted, lead to declines in investment spending, thus weakening demand and output, which caused unemployment to rise. Following this logic, proto-Keynesians asserted that governments can and should intervene in the private economy by increasing or reducing demand when necessary according to a counter-cyclical formula. They proposed that governments should increase government expenditure during periods of economic recession and reduce government expenditure during periods of economic prosperity.

The Keynesian logic led to the development of the field of macroeconomics that shifted the focus from individual or microlevel analysis of economic behavior to the aggregate behavior of economic actors within the country as a whole. Keynes and his followers asserted that it was possible for governments scientifically to study and predict economic shocks in advance of their occurrence. Keynes then proposed a variety of fiscal policy tools that governments could use to intervene and make adjustments to the economy.

Shortly thereafter, proto-Keynesian economists and economic policy-makers in both countries established what has become known as the *Keynesian welfare state* (KWS). The KWS entailed the development and continued expansion of "big government" and the modern welfare state that began with the New Deal and Beveridge political consensus in the United States and Britain. In the post-World War II era, governments in the United States and Britain placed a new emphasis on the importance of scientifically based economic advisory systems. As a result, that era witnessed the rise of economics research institutes, commissions, advisory committees, boards, and councils. In the mid-1960s to the mid-1970s, Keynes-oriented political-economic coalitions in both countries diligently pressed for the development of expert academic and policy institutes and official offices in government that were meant to institutionalize Keynesian policy beliefs. What resulted from their conscious efforts was of an intricate intellectual–political–policy network infrastructure that was driven by a Keynesian focus.

Over the years, the KWS led to an ever-growing public sector that included such entitlement institutions as Social Security and public assisted health care that would later require vast resources to maintain. The KWS would dominate the economic policy discourse for the next 40 years. Ultimately, the cost would outpace existing financial means, and that would lead to the creation of structural deficits and progressive tax systems. Over the next 30 years, the cost of supporting government programs would drive budget deficits in both the United States and Britain to crisis proportions. Stagflation and poor economic growth in the 1970s, combined with the rise of international capital mobility, caused politicians, constituents, policy bureaucrats, and academic advisors to rethink traditional policy beliefs that propelled new policy trajectories.

Under the leadership of Ronald Reagan, Margaret Thatcher, Bill Clinton, and Tony Blair, the major political parties in the United States and Britain, both progressive and conservative, have adopted broadly similar neoliberal fiscal policy views regarding the potential dangers of private disinvestment and slowed private sector growth related to bloated welfare states and uncontrolled public spending. We explore the various dimensions of the paradigm shift from Keynesian theory to neoliberalism in the United States and Britain through different partisan regimes over the course of nearly two decades. We explain Clinton and Blair's success in delivering balanced budgets and tax policies (consistent with balanced budget objectives) in the United States and Britain, something that Reagan and Thatcher could not achieve. The success in the 1990s of the New Left in consolidating and completing the neoliberal agenda under Clinton and Blair—initiated in the 1980s by the New Right under Reagan and Thatcher—is an important but tragically not very deeply analyzed phenomenon.

Despite the vast amount of work produced on the so-called Reagan–Thatcher Revolution, most accounts have ignored its broader significance in fundamentally reshaping how US and British policymakers and citizens think about budget deficits and welfare states in modern times. Although important and indispensable, previous studies have tended to focus rather narrowly on welfare retrenchment or programmatic reform in such areas as housing, labor markets, pensions schemes, and so on. Although such programmatic reforms may be important manifestations of neoliberal goals, they are only part of a larger "ideational" phenomenon that was directed more fundamentally at deconstructing the redistributive policy apparatus of the KWS that reigned in both countries from the 1930s and 1940s through the 1970s. We argue that the Reagan and Thatcher revolutions were as much about a paradigm shift in executive governance as they were about programmatic change. Both aspects are addressed here and are extended to the study of Clinton and Blair.

In a manner not seen in previous studies, we begin with an analysis of the essential components that underpinned the Reagan–Thatcher economic revolution. We explain how a shift from proto-Keynesian ideas toward neo-liberalism influenced the fiscal policy strategies of New Democrats and New Labour in both the White House and Whitehall. We point out that although Reagan, Thatcher, Clinton, and Blair demonstrated broadly similar neoliberal beliefs, each experienced varying degrees of success in his or her capacities to bring about policy change that were consistent with those broad neoliberal economic goals. In so doing, we provide a comprehensive account of the process by which executive leaders and other fiscal policy actors in the United States and Britain came to adopt broadly similar economic strategies. We analyze the diffusion of neoliberal ideas between successive governments that have different partisan colorations over the course of 20 years.

Chapter 1, entitled *Policy Ideas and Partisan Convergence,* and Chapter 2, entitled *Paradigms, Coalitions, and Directional Shifts in Economic Policy*, lay out the arguments regarding the influence of ideas in shaping policy change advanced in this book. Chapter 3, entitled *Deficit Reduction and Tax Reform in the Reagan–Thatcher Era*, dissects and explains differences between the neoliberal fiscal strategies pursued by Ronald Reagan and Margaret Thatcher. Chapter 4, entitled *Deficit Reduction and Tax Reform under Clinton and Blair*, compares and explains the remarkably similar fiscal policy strategies adopted under Bill Clinton and Tony Blair. Chapter 5 summarizes the key arguments advanced in this book as well as analyzes deficit reduction and tax reform in the current era.

Variations in fiscal policy strategies pursued by Reagan, Thatcher, Clinton, and Blair represent distinct experiments with neoliberalism. These distinct experiments are presented through a series of informative policy narratives that includes an account of the major movers and shakers that at first initiated and then later consolidated and completed the neoliberal fiscal revolution on the United States and Britain. We uncover the ideational motives that shaped the policy positions of critical players in the fiscal policy subsystem.

Acknowledgments

Although the authors take full responsibility for any mistakes or shortcomings that the reader may encounter in reading this book, we mention here a number of individuals to whom we are most grateful.

Ravi Roy expresses his sincere gratitude to his extraordinary coauthor, Art Denzau, for his limitless energies and dedication to this project. On a very personal note, Ravi Roy thanks his father, Ram M. Roy, for believing in his son. In addition, Ravi Roy acknowledges Mohit and Lia Nanda; Jitender and Jaya Roy; and Alec, Georgia, George, and Paul Gogonelis for all the love and support they provided over the years. I also extend a warm word to my fiancé, Joan, for the love and understanding that she showed throughout the trying period that one inevitably faces in finalizing a manuscript of this kind.

Ravi Roy also makes special mention here of a number of close friends, colleagues, and R.A.s who read and commented on various drafts or helped in the accumulation of data that were incorporated in the final version of this book. Many thanks to Nicholas Amponsah, Judy Liebman, Kevin Gerrity, Andy Hira, Darren Guerra, James Kaufman, Chris Styles, and Shelley Beroza.

Dr Arthur Denzau thanks his protégé (and now his colleague), Dr Ravi Roy, for his perseverance and vision in putting this book together. Both authors extend great appreciation to the Claremont Institute for Economic Policy Studies for its generous financial support of the project and especially to the Institute's director, Thomas D. Willett, for his faith in its merits. The authors jointly thank a number of our colleagues, including Tom Rochon, Nigel Boyle, Ronald Rogowski, Tom Borcherding, Peter Katzenstein, Roger Hayden, Peter Hall, Simon Lee, and Sven Steinmo. We also thank Paul Sabatier for his very helpful critique of early drafts of this book and for lessons regarding the importance of coalitions and subsystems that we gained by studying his Advocacy Coalition Framework.

We feel fortunate to have talked with policymakers in both the United States and Britain, conversations with whom offered valuable insights into how ideas influenced their policy goals. We appreciate the courtesy extended to us by members of the US Congress and by members of the Reagan and Clinton administrations. We feel compelled to mention a few by name, including Jim Miller III, William Niskanen, Robert Reich, Larry Summers, Richard Gephardt, Brad Sherman, and many others. In addition, we are indebted to a number of individuals who have played a significant role in shaping Britain's budgetary process in the modern times. That said, we mention and thank Andrew Maugham, Joe Grice, Andrew Kilpatrick, Ed Balls, Nigel Lawson, Matthew Seward, and Alan Manning for their conversations with us.

Abbreviations

AEI	American Enterprise Institute
BBC	British Broadcasting Corporation
BEA	Budget Enforcement Act
CBI	Confederation of British Industry
CEO	chief executive officer
CPRS	Central Policy Review Staff
CSR	Central Spending Review
DDC	Democratic deficit cutters
DLC	Democratic Leadership Council
DTI	Department of Trade and Industry
EITC	earned income tax credit
EMU	European Monetary Union
ERM	Exchange Rate Mechanism
ERTA	Economic Recovery Tax Act
EU	European Union
FY	fiscal year
G-7	Group of Seven
GDP	gross domestic product
GNP	gross national product
GRH	Gramm–Rudman–Hollings
HUD	Department of Housing and Urban Development
IRA	Individual Retirement Account
IMF	International Monetary Fund
IRS	Internal Revenue Service
KWS	Keynesian welfare state
MTFS	medium-term financial strategy
NASDAQ	National Association of Securities Dealers Automated Quotation System
NEC	National Economic Council
NEDC	National Economic Development Council
NHS	National Health Service
OBRA	Omnibus Budget Reconciliation Act
Ofgas	Office of Gas Supply

Oftel	Office of Telecommunications
Ofwat	Office of Water Services
OMB	Office of Management and Budget
PESC	Public Expenditure Survey Committee
PIU	Performance Innovation Unit

1 Policy ideas and partisan convergence

In most of the World War II era, it was typically assumed that left-of-center governments in the United States and Great Britain pursued economic policies that contributed to ever-growing increases in public spending and higher taxes. Right-of-center governments, by way of contrast, were normally assumed to support policies that reduced deficit spending and sought lower taxes. These characterizations were reinforced by the elections of Ronald Reagan and Margaret Thatcher and by their highly publicized crusade to reverse the wheels of "big government." Both leaders charged that the enormous welfare state and its twin redistributive engines—structural deficit spending and progressive taxation—were most directly responsible for the economic malaise that both countries experienced in the 1970s. Instituting broad reform proved to be a daunting task, as both leaders faced the formidable problem of convincing embedded interests to dismantle politically desirable public programs. By the end of their terms, both Reagan and Thatcher failed to cultivate the necessary political support required to complete the reforms they initially espoused.

Neoliberal factions began budding in the Democratic and Labour Parties in the United States and Britain in the 1980s. By the early 1990s, neoliberalism had captured the political mainstream in both parties. In the latter half of that decade, left-of-center governments, led by Bill Clinton and Tony Blair, were able to consolidate and complete critical aspects of the Reagan–Thatcher fiscal agenda. The purpose of this book is to analyze and explain how the "new left" led by Clinton and Blair adopted and successfully instituted neoliberal fiscal policies that facilitated balanced budgets, something the "new right" led by Reagan and Thatcher could not accomplish. The term *new left*, as it is used here, refers to left-of-center governments that ascended to power in the 1990s in the United States, Britain, Germany, the Netherlands, and Italy. Recent left-of-center governments led by Bill Clinton, Tony Blair, Gerhard Schroeder, Wim Kok, and Massimo D'Alema have become associated with a "third-way" approach to governance. That distinguishes them from their "traditional left" predecessors who were associated with the development and support of the Keynesian welfare state (KWS). The term *new left* should be read here in its international context.

This book has three main objectives. The first is to analyze and explain broad neoliberal convergence in fiscal policy goals among the Reagan, Thatcher, Clinton, and Blair governments. The second is to analyze the underlying core belief and secondary policy belief systems that shaped each government's distinct fiscal policy agendas and strategies. The third deals with a much more compelling, yet far more elusive, subject. It explains how Clinton and Blair ultimately succeeded in restructuring US and British tax and spending apparatuses in a manner that made it possible for them to balance their country's budgets, and it explains why their conservative predecessors could not achieve that.

Despite their many differences, the Tories and Labour in Britain, along with Democrats and Republicans in the United States, share a common objective—all four parties seek to win elections for the purpose of implementing their own brand of public policy. Of course, each does so in a manner that will enable them to maintain and expand their respective electoral bases. Partisan governments carrying any one of these labels will ultimately seek to influence a variety of redistributive policy and programs in a manner that will allow them to remain in power for as long as possible.[1] At critical junctures, they will even adopt policy ideas championed by their partisan opponents, albeit with their own programmatic slant and political reasoning. When governments of different partisan colorations embrace broadly similar policy ideas and strategies, we may refer to this phenomenon as *partisan convergence*. Partisan convergence is itself fundamentally rooted in a mutually shared set of policy beliefs or what may be termed a *policy paradigm*. Therefore, we examine how an interpartisan acceptance of Neoliberal ideas by United States and British policymakers shaped fiscal policy change in both countries from the 1980s to the present.

This book focuses on partisan convergence with respect to economic ideas because of such ideas' importance in shaping policy outcomes. The subject also occupies a central concern in the growing polemic over the future of left-of-center governments in the industrial democracies. The purpose here is to examine the ideational sources of the policy convergence that has occurred among left- and right-of-center governments in two specific pluralist democracies since the early 1980s. Partisan interests are derived through cognitive understandings of policy problems. When modes of thought change, traditional interest-based affiliations are often altered as a result. Recent changes in partisan choices are deeply rooted in a shift in dominant policy ideas.

The arguments advanced in this book regarding the influence of ideas on fiscal policy change in the United States and Britain are supported by a series of analytical narratives. We proceed on the basis of three broad conceptual hooks. (1) Although all four governments examined here sought to institute fiscal policy changes that were consistent with broad neoliberal economic principles and beliefs, significant distinctions between them are apparent and are thoroughly discussed. Reagan made tax relief in marginal rates his core fiscal policy concern and deficit reduction an important, but secondary, policy issue. Thatcher, on the other hand, made deficit reduction her core fiscal policy concern and tax reform an important, but secondary, policy issue. In Chapter 3, a series of case studies is presented in support of the proposition that differences between Reagan's and Thatcher's fiscal policy strategies were based on the fact that each held distinct core policy beliefs. Reagan and his supporters, for example, adopted a unique mix of Laffer-curve supply-side economic ideas that incorporated elements of traditional conservatism. (2) Much like Thatcher, and unlike Reagan, the Clinton and Blair governments made deficit reduction their core fiscal policy concern and regarded tax reform as an important, but secondary, issue. In the subsequent chapters of this book, evidence is presented that supports the conclusion that both the Clinton and Blair governments embraced a highly similar set of monetarist beliefs. (3) The new right, led by Reagan and Thatcher, initiated the neoliberal fiscal revolution. Later, this was synthesized and carried to fruition under the new left, at first by Clinton and subsequently by Blair. Our discussion of each of the four leaders reveals discrete experiments of the revolution itself.

Policy ideas, policy learning, and policy subsystems are critical concepts used to explore the varying dimensions of the neoliberal paradigm and its impact on tax and spending policies in the United States and Britain over the last 20 years. Paradigms (cognitive frameworks) define problems and methods for solving them. Dominant paradigms are subverted as anomalies accumulate. Only when an alternative paradigm emerges and better explains these anomalies can broad change occur in the discourse. Therefore, "… a policy paradigm shift results from the accretion of anomalies, contestation, and the replacement of one paradigm by another set of ideas."[2]

Major policy shifts involve fundamental alterations in policy ideas, goals, and strategies. In explaining how this process works, Peter Hall's explanation of policy paradigms and major shifts in policy is highly useful.[3] Hall distinguishes three levels of policy change. First-order changes are mainly incremental in nature and are normally associated with routine decision making by bureaucratic elites; they usually occur in the absence of any interference from such outside pressures as interest groups and other societal actors. Second-order changes go one step further in that they usually involve the development of new policy instruments and entail changes in strategic action but do not significantly alter the basic goals that inform the policies themselves. According to Hall, first- and second-order changes can be characterized as "normal policymaking" that takes place without challenging the overall terms of an existing policy paradigm. Third-order changes, however, involve dramatic shifts in the actual goals and basic causal assumptions of policy problems and the appropriate solutions; they entail alterations of core assumptions and beliefs over how the economy functions and operates. Changes occurring at this level normally involve a wide group of political actors involved in the policy subsystem. A policy subsystem usually encompasses a large and diverse set of actors that attempt to translate their beliefs pertaining to a particular political issue or set of issues into state action.[4]

Given the number of actors involved in large policy arenas, such as deficit reduction and tax reform, it is necessary to organize groups of actors into manageable units of analysis.[5] Policy subsystems are composed of elites that operate as interest groups, agency officials, legislators, executive leaders, intellectuals, and 'policy wonks' (highly specialized policy experts and technocrats) who are brought into a common policy arena by virtue of the fact that they share a general set of normative causal beliefs over an issue.[6] In most cases, subsystems contain only a few politically significant coalitions that are continually competing for policy dominance.[7] Policy subsystems (1) are guided by a set of ideas, (2) communicate through a policy discourse, and (3) are composed of a few distinct coalitions that seek to affect policy outcomes in a manner consistent with their causal beliefs and collective objectives. Cognitive as well as political factors are important in shaping the behavior of decision makers.

A policy paradigm is simply a particular set of shared beliefs that guide the efforts of subsystem actors.[8] Policy subsystems and the coalitions that comprise them are organized around a set of core values and policy strategies.[9] In examining areas of fiscal policy, such as deficit reduction and tax reform, it is appropriate to place special emphasis on the role of executive leadership. When partisan administrations converge over policy ideas, there is strong evidence that a paradigm shift has occurred. We study how the Clinton and Blair administrations were able to bring about meaningful change in the areas of deficit reduction and tax reform by examining the role of executive leaders in the fiscal policy subsystems. Having done so, we are able to identify the structural aspects that lie at the root of their respective budgetary successes and failures.

Dissecting the neoliberal paradigm shift

Neoliberalism, as a policy paradigm, is a political application of liberal economics-based thinking; it emphasizes individual initiative, the role of incentives, and market-oriented solutions. The neoliberal paradigm is embedded in a set of classic economic ideas that favor market mechanisms in allocating valued resources among alternative uses.[10] Andrew Gamble describes the essence of neoliberalism in the United States and Britain:

> The new ascendancy of the doctrines of economic liberalism in Anglo-America in the 1970s and 1980s created some confusion for ideological labels. Proponents of the new liberalism were often forced to describe themselves as conservatives, in order not to be confused with supporters of collectivism and the extended state, which is what the term "liberal"

had come to signify ... The convergence of conservative and libertarian positions from the late 1960s onwards in Britain and the United States was widely described as constituting a "New Right" which spawned a considerable literature from both supporters and critics ... The emergence of the New Right as an intellectual phenomenon in the form of various think-tanks, journals and publications and as a phenomenon in the shape of the Thatcher Government in Britain and the Reagan Government in the United States was a key ideological event in Anglo-America in the second half of the twentieth century.[11]

The different partisan leaderships under examination embraced distinct elements of the neoliberal paradigm. In examining the neoliberal revolution from the period of Reagan–Thatcher to that of Clinton–Blair, it is useful to identify the distinct strands that have comprised it. These strands include Laffer supply-side economics, monetarism, and traditional conservatism.[12] Each is based on a distinct set of core policy beliefs. Policy preferences, priorities, and strategies adopted by subsystem actors are causally related to their core beliefs and understandings about how the economy works. Laffer-curve supply-side economics, monetarism, and traditional conservatism may all be considered "supply-side" in the broad sense that they focus on the microside of economics by emphasizing policies that promote individual entrepreneurial growth and productivity. The mutual underpinning of these distinct strands is "a common belief in the efficiency and optimality of free markets and, as a corollary, a determined opposition to Keynesian policies and demand management."[13]

Michael Boskin brings out that monetarists in the Reagan administration, for example, were concerned first and foremost with tighter and more stable money and sought to promote policies that would produce disinflation. Traditional free-market conservatives emphasized the need for fiscal restraint and, therefore, focused on limiting the growth of domestic spending. Laffer-curve supply-siders, by way of contrast, distinguished themselves by focusing on marginal tax rates and investment incentives.

Laffer-curve supply-side economics, which carried more weight in the United States than in Britain, may be distinguished from the two "mainstream supply-side schools": traditional conservatism and monetarism. William Niskanen brings out that Laffer-curve supply-side economics "does not address the effects of government borrowing; specifically, it does not provide a basis for concluding that deficits do not matter."[14] Although monetarism stresses that actual output can fall below potential output in cases where demand is insufficient to employ productive resources fully, Laffer-curve supply-side economics assumes that aggregate demand always adjusts to aggregate supply.[15] Since Laffer-curve supply-siders believed that the money supply adapts to market pressures as does any other supply, they did not share the same conservative and monetarist concerns and sense of urgency regarding the budget deficit.[16]

Laffer-curve supply-side economics began to surface in the mid-1970s and was promulgated by a relatively small but cohesive group of economists and politicians who believed that high economic growth was dependent on "freeing-up" the amount of capital available for private investment.[17] This would be achieved, along with improving incentives to produce wealth, they argued, by significantly reducing the level of taxation on private income. The dilemma for elected politicians in Congress was to devise a way to reduce taxes while at the same time preserving politically popular (and often expensive) social programs. The supply-side logic held that the "growth in the economy produced by new investment would be sufficiently strong to yield net gains in tax revenues."[18]

Monetarism emphasizes that the amount of money in circulation is the most important factor in determining price levels in the economy.[19] Monetarists assert that monetary rather than fiscal policy is the appropriate instrument for keeping inflation under control. They hold the view that Keynesian fiscal policy does "nothing to alter the underlying 'natural' rate of unemployment in an economy."[20] Monetarists further maintain that over the long term, stable low unemployment could be achieved only if government committed itself to pursuing modest and predictable rates of growth in its money supply.[21] According to the monetarist logic, supply will produce its own demand, thus "leaving no gap between potential and real output other than that attributed to frictional market adjustments."[22]

Traditional economic conservatism gained prominence in the 1970s as the level of government intervention and the size of state budgets had been enormously increasing in the face of waning economic growth. Many of the basic assumptions rooted in traditional conservatism are highly consistent with monetarism. Monetarists and traditional conservatives agree on the need for tighter money and cuts in domestic spending. At the same time, traditional conservatives were aligned with the Laffer-curve supply-siders on the need for tax reform. The core focus of traditional conservatives, however, was reducing the size of the deficit that had more than tripled under the conservative leadership of President Reagan. Traditional conservatives assert that deficit spending not only "crowds out" private capital but helps to create economic conditions that lead to dramatic rises in inflation.

The Clinton–Blair era

If one is successfully to make the case that a paradigm shift has indeed occurred, one must be prepared to demonstrate that neoliberal economic ideas have shaped the policy strategies of successive partisan governments. The Clinton and Blair governments were part of a neoliberal consensus that followed a combination of traditional conservative and monetarist principles. We conduct a comparative examination of Clinton's and Blair's fiscal policies and the ideas that inspired them.

The Clinton administration's achievements in reforming welfare, eliminating the budget deficit, and reducing the overall size of the federal government was a major part of a retrenchment effort that Reagan had begun but was largely unable to complete. In the same way, Blair's adherence to the spending limits established by his Tory (an abbreviation used commonly for the main Conservative Party) predecessors provides strong evidence of neoliberal legitimacy in the post-Thatcher era.

By the time Clinton came to power in 1993, Laffer-curve supply-side economics had lost a good deal of credibility with policymakers in the United States. Herbert Stein states that "while there are still people who believed that this prescription worked, or that it would have worked if it were followed more rigorously or if Congress had not interfered, the number of true believers in the extreme version of the supply-side approach has surely diminished."[23] This was due mainly to Reagan's inability to control the enormous growth in deficit spending that had occurred throughout the 1980s (and continued into the 1990s under George H. Bush).

By the early to mid-1990s, the deficit issue emerged as a salient and ubiquitous concern among politicians and voters on both sides of the political spectrum. This was driven by a series of important developments. Hardcore deficit cutters, who embraced some combination of monetarist and conservative ideas, had successfully framed the deficit issue as the leading cause of declining investment and unsatisfactory economic performance. Leading deficit reduction advocates in the United States, such as Bill Clinton and Alan Greenspan, were convinced that declining investment stemmed directly from disparities between long-term and short-term interest rates caused by the enormous size of the public debt. As discussed fully in Chapter 4, interest on the total debt in the United States and Britain became a major concern among the voting public in the two countries.

The five main arguments of the book

Regarding the influence of ideas in shaping major shifts in fiscal policy in the United States and Britain, five related arguments are advanced in this book:

• A neoliberal paradigm shift in the fiscal policy subsystem has occurred in the United States and Britain since the 1980s.
• Partisan convergence in the United States and Britain is both strongly indicative of, and intrinsically related to, a broad shift in the reigning paradigm governing a policy subsystem.
• Differences in the neoliberal fiscal policy strategies pursued by the Reagan and Thatcher administrations reflect differences in their core and secondary policy beliefs.
• Striking similarities in the fiscal policy strategies pursued by the Clinton and Blair administrations reflect their mutual commitment to similar core policy beliefs.

- The ability of Clinton and Blair to consolidate and complete the neoliberal fiscal paradigm shift that was initiated by Reagan and Thatcher was rooted in heresthetics.[24]

A neoliberal paradigm shift in the fiscal policy subsystem has occurred in the United States and Britain since the 1980s

In analyzing policy ideas and outcomes over time through a chronicled comparison of the Reagan and Thatcher governments with the Clinton and Blair administrations, we are able to present historical-empirical evidence that a transpartisan consensus over economic ideas has occurred in the two countries. Major, or third-order, paradigm changes often occur under the following conditions:

- The reigning paradigm fails to anticipate and explain critical anomalies.
- A radical shift occurs in the hierarchy of goals guiding policy.[25]
- A radical shift occurs in the discourse employed by policy makers and in the analysis of the economy on which policy is based.
- Advocates in a subsystem successfully translate the policy cores and the secondary aspects of their belief systems into concrete budgetary reforms (Figures 1.1, 1.2).

By the mid-1980s, national-level economic policy makers in both the United States and Britain had widely accepted the belief that economic growth was dependent on encouraging greater private investment. These new policy views reflected a shift in the policy discourse that now focused on reforming progressive tax structures and pursuing fiscal prudence. The United States and Britain both experienced enduring periods of slow growth and economic malaise throughout the 1960s and 1970s in the presence of ever-growing public expenditures. This experience led policymakers in both countries to conclude that the basic redistributive logic on which the preexisting tax and spending structures were based was fundamentally flawed. They viewed the twin redistributive engines of big deficits and excessive predation on capital wealth to be the root causes of disinvestment and slow economic growth in the two countries. Neoliberals on both sides of the Atlantic, therefore, advocated more investment-friendly tax codes in tandem with cuts in existing levels of public spending to relieve pressure on the budget deficit. Although neoliberals themselves continued to argue over which area of fiscal policy was in need of the greatest attention, most agreed that major reform in both areas was required for liberating capital for new private investment. We demonstrate in Chapters 3 and 4 that by the early 1990s, these views came to dominate the policy mainstream in the two countries.

Hall's policy paradigm model and the
policy subsystems approach

- Dominant policy paradigm fails to anticipate
  and explain anomalous events (mid-1970s
  stagflation).

- Shift in hierarchy of policy goals (from full
  employment to low inflation).

- A radical shift in policy instruments occurs.

- Radical shift in policy discourse occurs
  (from KWS to neoliberalism).

- Exogenous change in socioeconomic
  conditions provided for the rise of new
  ideas and coalitions.

- Core aspects of belief systems of
  dominant coalition in the subsystem are
  translated into programmatic outcomes.

**Major shift in
fiscal policy**
(partisan convergence)

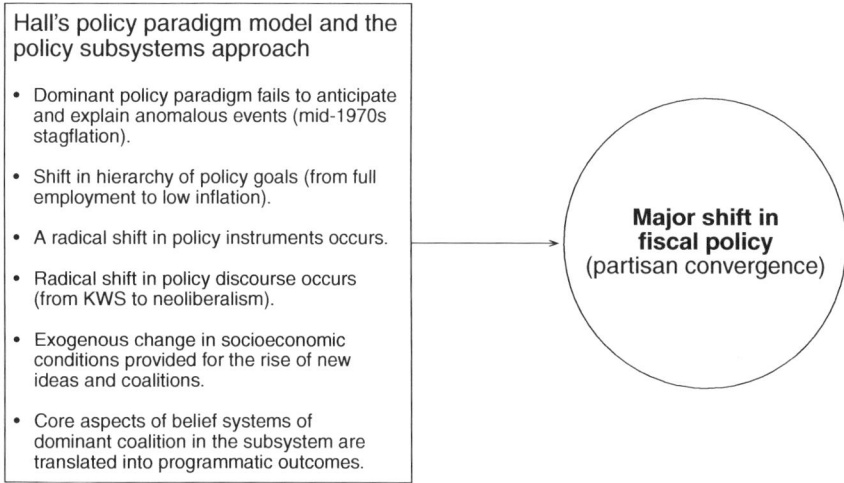

Figure 1.1 The ideas-based framework of analysis

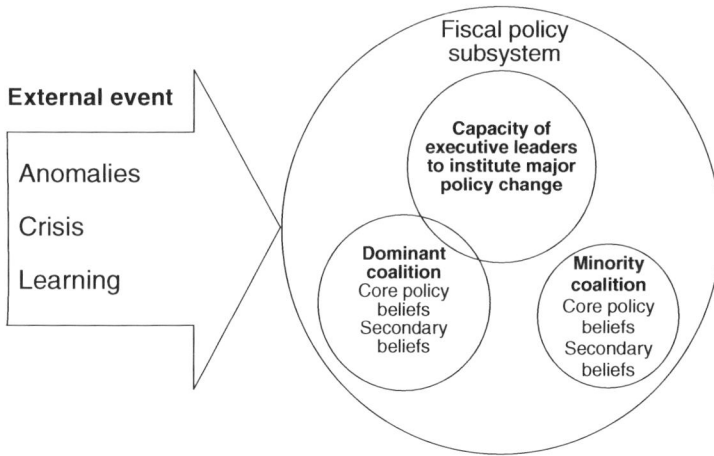

External event

Anomalies

Crisis

Learning

Fiscal policy
subsystem

**Capacity of
executive leaders
to institute major
policy change**

**Dominant
coalition**
Core policy
beliefs
Secondary
beliefs

**Minority
coalition**
Core policy
beliefs
Secondary
beliefs

Figure 1.2 Executive leaders, coalitions, and policy change

Partisan convergence in the United States and Britain is both strongly indicative of, and intrinsically related to, a broad shift in the reigning paradigm governing a policy subsystem

Chapter 2 provides a detailed explanation of how neoliberal ideas were introduced into the elite economic policy-making structures in the United States and Britain in the 1980s. Under the leaderships of Reagan and Thatcher, neoliberalism-oriented economists were appointed to key economic policy positions in the Treasury and Office of Management and Budget (OMB) in the case of the United States and in the Treasury in Britain. The fact that governments of various partisan persuasions in the United States and Britain adopted broadly similar neoliberal economic policy ideas and goals during the same historical period is compelling, given sharp differences in the relative size of their economies and in the configuration of their political-institutional arrangements.

Timing was also a critical factor in driving change. Major policy change requires a decade or more to allow for what Paul Sabatier refers to as the "enlightenment function" of policy research.[26] A decade or more is usually enough time for policy to undergo at least one full cycle of formulation, implementation, evaluation, and reformulation. New policy ideas and the policies that stem from them often meet with formidable opposition from embedded status-quo interests and other contending coalitions. "The sense of urgency over the deficit was heightened by a public dialogue that had sharpened over the course of a decade. The deficit had become a powerful symbol of what was wrong in American [and British] government."[27]

The rejection of the Keynesian welfare state (KWS) paradigm and the rise of neoliberalism in the United States and Britain has been a long-term process that occurred over the course of nearly two decades. Baumgartner and Jones argue convincingly that "over the long term, policy making is characterized by change in public understandings of policy problems and in the institutions that vie for policy control. In pluralist systems, the interaction of image and venue allows for rapid changes in policy outputs during some periods and for prolonged stability during others."[28] Policy change, therefore, is ultimately driven by "a redefinition of policy problems."[29]

Differences in fiscal policy strategies pursued by the Reagan and Thatcher administrations reflect differences in their core policy beliefs

Although they shared a common set of *deep core normative beliefs* (i.e., the belief in market efficiency and reducing the size of government), the Reagan, Thatcher, Clinton, and Blair governments have pursued distinct neoliberal policy strategies. The discrete strategies pursued each by these four governments reflect differences in their core and secondary *policy belief* systems. Although core aspects of a belief system represent the most pressing concerns of executive leaders and the coalitions of which they are a part, secondary aspects of a belief system are also very important. Executive leaders will make every attempt to institutionalize secondary aspects of their belief systems so long as they do not come into direct conflict with core aspects. That said, an individual or group's core policy beliefs will most often influence secondary aspects of their belief system and the overall range of policy alternatives that they may consider.

Divergent neoliberal policy strategies pursued by Reagan and Thatcher reflect the different priorities of the two leaders regarding the level of importance of tax reform versus fiscal-monetary stability. Reagan's steadfast belief in Laffer-curve supply-side economic principles and his belief that excessive government predation was the root cause of poor economic performance impelled him to pursue tax reduction as the core issue and deficit reduction as an important, but secondary, issue in his neoliberal agenda. By way of contrast, Thatcher's core belief in the merits of fiscal prudence encouraged her to pursue deficit reduction as the core issue and tax reform as an important, but secondary, issue, of her neoliberal agenda. The varied neoliberal strategies pursued by the Reagan and Thatcher administrations represent different dimensions of the neoliberal paradigm shift in the United States and Britain in the 1980s. Table 1.1 illustrates each administration's core and secondary policy beliefs and corresponding policy preferences.

Under certain critical conditions, executive leaders (and other subsystem actors) may be compelled to concede secondary aspects of their policy beliefs to realize or further core aspects. Whenever possible, however, they will seek to institute secondary aspects of their policy beliefs. This point is illustrated by the fact that although he treated the deficit issue with a certain "benign neglect" in the first years of his presidency, Reagan revisited the deficit problem once key aspects of his tax reform agenda had been successfully instituted. His administration insisted, for example, that the 1986 tax reforms be revenue-neutral in an effort to reduce pressure on the budget deficit. Although she raised the value-added tax and imposed new taxes on North Sea oil revenues in accordance with her core commitment to alleviate deficit spending, Thatcher simultaneously supported significant tax cuts on upper-income individuals in accordance with her secondary commitment to reducing the tax burden on individual private wealth.

Striking similarities in the fiscal policy strategies pursued by the Clinton and Blair administrations reflect their mutual acceptance of similar core policy beliefs

Moderate members of the Democratic Party in the Democratic Leadership Council and modernizers in the Labour Party believed that modern governments needed to commit themselves to fiscal prudence to attract new financial capital investment. The Clinton and Blair governments, therefore, made deficit reduction (and hence spending prudence) the central issues in their overall economic agendas. The tax reform strategies pursued by Clinton and Blair were forged in accordance with the overarching goal of maintaining fiscal prudence. Believing fiscal stability to be the key factor for bringing down long-term interest rates, Clinton and Blair, much like Thatcher and unlike Reagan, consciously sought to limit tax cuts to specific areas in a manner that would not jeopardize deficit reduction goals. In that vein, both the Clinton and Blair governments sought to provide targeted tax relief for small business, long-term investors, capital investment in research and development, and emerging service sector-based development.

Table 1.1 Executive leaders and different dimensions of the neoliberal paradigm shift

Leader	Core beliefs	Secondary beliefs	Core policy issue	Secondary policy issue
Reagan, core partisan supporters (Laffer-supply-side tax cutters)	Government inefficient; government predation trigger to poor economic performance	Monetary and fiscal stability necessary for economic growth	Seeks to restrict extent of predation through minimal taxation	Seeks overall stability through deficit reduction and spending restraint
Thatcher, core partisan supporters (Tory neoliberals, Tory drys [monetarist-deficit cutters])	Government inefficient; monetary and fiscal stability necessary for economic growth	Government predation forerunner of poor economic performance	Seeks overall stability through deficit reduction and spending restraint	Seeks to restrict the extent of predation through minimal taxation
Clinton, Blair, core bipartisan supporters (traditional conservatives, deficit cutters)	Purpose of government to provide an economic environment of fiscal and monetary stability; investment in human and financial capital key for growth	Economic growth encouraged by government investment in human and financial capital by reducing the tax burdens on certain economic behavior	Monetary stability encouraged by investment; seek overall stability through deficit reduction and spending restraint	Seek to offer tax credits and tax relief for investment in research and development, small business, and education

The ability of Clinton and Blair to consolidate and complete the neoliberal fiscal paradigm shift initiated by Reagan and Thatcher was rooted in heresthetics

Presidential and prime ministerial administrations seeking to institute fundamental policy changes must secure a political mandate from key actors within
a given policy subsystem.[30] Stated differently, broad shifts in national-level
fiscal policy are facilitated by executive leaders who are able to build support
for their agendas among latent or potential sympathizers in a policy subsystem.
Executives who are able to frame policy issues in a manner that enables them
to build broad coalitional support within the policy subsystem can facilitate
dramatic shifts in national fiscal policy.

It would be tautological to assert that dominant coalitions in a policy
subsystem attained their hegemony by virtue of the fact that they were
"successful" in institutionalizing their core beliefs. One must provide a more
precise explanation for this success. Successful executives (and the coalitions
they may lead) are characterized by their ability to drastically reshape a policy
discourse (and thus the range of policy alternatives that may be seriously
considered) in a manner consistent with their own core and secondary beliefs.
Executive leaders can play a pivotal role in mobilizing coalition members
toward a common cause. Their success lies in their ability to frame policy
problems and solutions in a manner that enables them to mobilize the
maximum number of "potential core supporters" in a subsystem in support
of their cause without compromising core aspects of their belief system.
Their ability to accomplish this is rooted in what William Riker, a founder
of modern positive political analysis, refers to as *heresthetics*. Heresthetic is
concerned with the "strategy value" of language, symbols, and political
framing used by executive leaders to mobilize support for others to join
them in alliances and coalitions.[31] It has to do with the art of framing policy
problems and solutions in a manner that enables executive leaders and their
coalition allies to expand political support for their causal views and policy
agendas without compromising core aspects of their policy belief system.

Reagan, Thatcher, Clinton, and Blair are dynamic partisan leaders who
have used their executive power (both formal and informal) to mobilize
political coalitions toward broad neoliberal change. Riker asserts that a pivotal
advantage of being an executive leader or the leader of a legislative body is
"that they have considerable control over the agenda, sometimes even enough
control to determine which motions, bills, amendments, and so on are
approved."[32] Although popular leaders can exert substantial influence in
setting policy agenda by drawing awareness to an issue, the successful adoption
of public policy still requires building broader support in a subsystem.

Clinton and Blair were remarkably successful in reframing several conservative policy issues in a manner that has become palatable to the center-left
in the United States and Britain. They have built a new coalition that has
incorporated many individuals from the traditional left (i.e., members of

organized labor) as well as groups normally associated with the center-right (i.e., business groups) by pursuing a "third-way" strategy. Additionally, they sought the crucial support of the middle class along with large and small business. By the early- to mid-1990s, both middle-class and business groups in the United States and Britain had grown disillusioned with the conservative leadership of Reagan–Bush and Thatcher–Major and their inability to control the deficit and effectively to cut "extravagant and wasteful" welfare spending. They were further disenchanted with conservative executive leaders and their inability to adopt economic strategies that would build confidence in the economy through a satisfactory deficit reduction strategy. Clinton's resolute commitment to reducing the size of the deficit was motivated by his devotion both to promoting stability in the bond market and financial sectors of the economy and to "helping the middle-class, the working families, those who had voted for him."[33]

Martin Walker brings out that "genuinely a new Democrat, Clinton believed that the liberal, welfare reforms of the 1960s were well-intentioned, but had rotten results. He sincerely wanted to end the dependency culture of welfare, to espouse fiscal discipline, and cut the deficit."[34] These beliefs were the foundation of both Clinton and Blair's centrist neoliberal agenda aimed at dismantling the traditional redistributive welfare state while seeking to modernize labor markets by providing new opportunities to help individuals to maximize their job skill potential. That agenda uniquely combined *welfare-to-work* policies (or workfare) with free trade; supported increases in the minimum wage while providing tax cuts for small business; and expanded income tax credits for the working poor while cutting off benefits to career welfare seekers. Heightened public awareness made it easier in the mid-1990s for policy makers and the public alike to accept neoliberal change than it was in the early 1980s. In the following chapters, we show how neoliberal ideas and strategies had an opportunity to become more fully developed, allowing them to settle into the policy discourse mainstream over the course of nearly two decades.

Drawbacks of prevailing causal explanations of partisan convergence

In this section, we examine the weaknesses inherent in the international relations (IR)-based and (pure) rational-choice (interest-based) explanations. Contending political economy explanations of partisan convergence in economic policy are important and illuminating but require greater refinement. They fail to explain in exact terms how globalization, internationalization, financial integration, or the like directly produced partisan convergence in economic policy making. Therefore, they are of little use in helping us to identify specific sources of policy change within particular countries.

Weaknesses in pure international relations (IR)-based explanations

The first explanation centers on international sources of partisan convergence. This is known as the *efficiency* argument.[35] The efficiency argument applies the basic tenets of the "international capital mobility hypothesis"[36] to argue that the competitive imperatives posed by growing global interdependence are expected to compel domestic governments (regardless of partisan persuasion) toward "cutting government expenditure, aggressively pursuing smaller budget deficits, and adopting lower rates of capital taxation."[37] The efficiency explanation posits that growing capital mobility has led to the dismantling of various social policies and programs the initial development and continued expansion of which have traditionally been associated with left-of-center governments.[38] Those who advance the efficiency argument assert that left-of-center governments have had to adopt new policy positions and initiatives to survive in a world increasingly being shaped by global imperatives.

Following this logic, modern governments, whether they belong to the left or the right of center, have a mutual incentive to "rationalize" their tax systems and limit public spending to create financial environments that allow them to compete successfully for increasingly mobile capital. This argument lies at the center of a growing debate in political and economic circles regarding how increasing "internationalization in its many forms and guises affects government policies."[39] Mark Hallerberg and Williams Roberts Clark concisely explain the major contentions of the globalization debate:

> Many of the models and discussions either implicitly or explicitly argue that increasing capital mobility will cause many of the changes to the capabilities and size of the nation-state. Governments lose some level of autonomy over policy because the "invisible hand" of capital movements rewards those states that pursue capital-friendly policies and punishes those states that favor other factors of production. In its most extreme form some predict that "globalization" more generally will spell the end of the nation-state as the discipline of international markets replaces the government as the ultimate policy maker on economic issues. Others, while perhaps seeing some role for the nation-state in the future, believe that certain policy options will no longer be available in a world of increasing economic integration.[40]

According to globalization scholars, partisan-based prerogatives are expected to diminish in this constrictive environment. Therefore, the policies that the (traditional) left-of-center proponents had supported and on which they had developed an electoral allegiance would increasingly be threatened in the face of globalization pressures. There are numerous problems, however, in applying this explanation to the case of partisan convergence in the United

States and Britain. The efficiency argument fails to explain why left- and right-of-center governments in both the United States and Britain, the economies of which were exposed to very different international constraints, nonetheless pursued very similar neoliberal economic policies since the 1980s. It seems counterintuitive to suggest that international pressures could easily trump domestic pressures and concerns in shaping fiscal policy outcomes in a large country such as the United States, given its enormous internal market, economies of scale, and hegemonic status. In the three previous decades, governments belonging to both parties in the United States had continued to borrow and spend at record levels with apparently little fear of capital flight. Therefore, the globalization argument provides an incomplete account of what drove policy makers on both sides of the political fence to adopt neoliberal fiscal goals. The efficiency argument fails to provide us with any systematic explanation of how globalization caused policymakers to reexamine their existing economic policies and strategies.

Domestic impulsions seem to have a greater effect over the size and shape of Britain's economic policy destiny as well. Although Britain's economy remains more integrated into the international financial system than any of its G-7 competitors when measured in terms of inward and outward investment as a share of gross domestic product (GDP), Britain's business cycle has been running in a direction independent of Europe's largest players, such as France and Germany.[41] In pursuing its independent fiscal and monetary course, Britain was able to escape the enduring inflation problem that continued to plague these major European countries throughout the whole of the 1990s.[42] Britain averted the threat of rapidly rising inflation in 1997 by keeping interest rates (approximately) two percent higher than the rest of the European Union, where they remained for more than a year despite European pressures for their immediate reduction.[43] The prevalence of domestic forces in affecting Britain's economic policies was apparent in John Major's decision to withdraw from the Exchange Rate Mechanism (ERM) in 1992. In withdrawing from the ERM, Major sought to reclaim Britain's domestic institutional prerogatives, although doing so re-exposed the pound to substantial movements against the German mark. Major's decision was a provocative demonstration of Britain's resilient state capacity.

More recently, many have argued that Britain's £118.2 billion balance of payments deficit has made it especially vulnerable to exchange rate movements that could lead to a potential crisis.[44] Given this, Britain's decision to put off joining the European Monetary Union (EMU) is especially interesting. It is, after all, commonly argued that internationally mobile foreign investors would prefer investing in EMU member countries on the assumption that the *Eurozone* would be the best guarantor of stable exchange rates and lower transaction costs. For most of the last decade, however, Germany and France have been aggressively moving toward the single currency, while "Britain has become increasingly detached from the idea, with no visible effect on the pattern of foreign direct investment."[45] In fact, foreign direct investment in Britain rose from $20b a year in the mid-1990s to $80b a year in 2001.[46] During the same period, it rose only from $24b to $39b a year in France and from $12b to $27b in Germany.[47] The Blair government's decision to postpone EMU entry against strong urgings by France and Germany presents a clear example both of Britain's willingness and of her ability to place domestic concerns regarding inflation ahead of "international pressures."[48]

There are additional problems with using the efficiency argument to explain partisan convergence in fiscal policy. Eric Helleiner and Louis Pauly argue convincingly that it was states themselves that "paved the road" toward globalization. Helleiner in particular emphasizes the participatory role of states in removing restrictions on the activities of financial market actors as well as opting not to impose stronger capital controls.[49] State actors did not use such instruments despite the fact that they possessed the legal authority and technical ability to have done so.[50] Given this, it is clear that while international forces may constrain policy choices and may in some cases even hasten the pace of policy change, they provide an incomplete causal explanation for the substance and direction of policy outcomes in the United States and Britain.[51] One must, therefore, consider additional causal explanations for the convergence.

Weaknesses in pure rational choice explanations

This book improves on (pure) rational-choice accounts that regard partisan convergence to be a solely Downsian or "median voter"-driven phenomenon. This Downsian explanation assumes that political parties, and hence partisan governments, will simply adopt similar policy positions and political rhetoric once a winning platform is discovered.[52] Although it might help us in determining what (electoral) incentives may have encouraged the Clinton and Blair administrations to move to the right in their policy objectives, the Downsian explanation fails to explain patterns of success and failure among partisan regimes. Pure rational-choice explanations suggest that if any change in the economic discourse did in fact occur, it was nothing more than political "flak" rather than a genuine shift in causal core beliefs. Rather, they argue that right-of-center governments led by Reagan and Thatcher simply used "idea rhetoric" as a justification "to do what they were going to do anyway." This group asserts that neoliberalism was used to justify politically desirable tax cuts and dissolution of expensive welfare programs. Under this logic, although they possessed no actual philosophical commitment to them, Clinton and Blair simply adopted these popular issues to win votes. Although we do not dispute the importance of electoral incentives in influencing the way in which policy issues are framed and pursued, the role of ideas in shaping the content and substance of policy can ill afford to be passed off as an epiphenomenon. Judith Goldstein and Robert Keohane give a concise summary of the rationalist critique of ideas and policy:

...in modern political economy and in international relations the impressive elaboration of rationalist explanations of behavior has called into question old assumptions about whether the substantive content of people's ideas really matters for policy. To many economists, and to political scientists captivated by their modes of thinking, ideas are unimportant or epiphenomenal either because agents correctly anticipate the results of their actions or because some selective process ensures that only agents who behave as though they were rational succeed. In such functional arguments, effects explain causes through rational anticipation and natural selection. The extreme version of this argument is that ideas are just hooks: competing elites seize on popular ideas to propagate and to legitimize their interests, but the ideas themselves do not play a causal role.[53]

There are critical flaws in the basic assumptions underlying the pure interest-based explanation and its treatment of ideas in the policy process. Goldstein and Keohane "challenge the explanatory power [of the pure rational-choice explanation] by suggesting the existence of empirical anomalies that can only be resolved when ideas are taken into account."[54] Arthur Denzau and Douglass North assert convincingly that rational behavior is itself determined by the information one possesses when making decisions.[55] Goldstein and Keohane confirm that ideas influence policy when "(1) the principled or causal beliefs they embody provide road maps that increase actors' clarity about goals or ends-means relationships, (2) when they affect outcomes of strategic situations in which there is no unique equilibrium, and (3) when they become imbedded in political institutions."[56] Consequently, the notion of "utility" itself is ultimately realized through a set of ideas and beliefs of what furthers one's interest and what does not.[57] This is not to suggest, of course, that interests are irrelevant; indeed, interests are vital to understanding allocation preferences. Rather, our argument is simply that ideas are an integral component in determining how groups perceive their interests.[58]

Politics, ideas, and partisan governance

Ideas are mental understandings and conceptions of both what is desirable and how actions relate to outcomes in the world. They "are manifested in beliefs, attitudes, values, and purposive actions."[59] Ideas and interests are discussed as distinct but related phenomena. Ideas are viewpoints about politics and economics that are presented into the policy-making process by actors who operate through policy subsystems. Rationalistic analysis "typically stipulates, but does not explain, individuals' preference for some outcome."[60] Therefore, if we are to understand how preferences over policies are formed, "we need to understand what ideas are available and how policymakers choose among them."[61] Causal beliefs determine policy goals and priorities along with the strategies that will be used to attain their objectives.[62]

Focusing on ideas can help us to understand better why "new Labour" in Britain and "new Democrats" in the United States adopted policy choices that would normally be expected to offend their "traditional constituencies," namely organized labor and the "working poor." Ultimately, we see ideas to be the critical dynamic of both policy change and continuity. The manner in which ideas are introduced into the political arena shapes partisan debates concerning policy agendas and goals. Accordingly, we believe partisan convergence ultimately stems from a "rethinking" of the current assumptions regarding what sorts of policies produce sustainable levels of economic growth and which do not. It entailed a new thinking regarding the power of economic growth to improve the lot of all, not just elite classes or other subsets of the population. This is an important point because governments belonging to either the left or the right of center will always want to preside over a thriving economy so as to ensure their party's survival in the next election.

The role of ideas in shaping policy problems and solutions

Economic ideas on their own are latent resources that must be championed by policy advocates if they are to be converted into purposeful political action. This development should not be confused with political "flak." Ideas are at the root of these rationales themselves and ultimately shape the configuration of policy choices that will be considered.[63] Economic ideas shape the conceivable alternatives that can be considered, thereby establishing the dimensions of the policy debate. Over the last century, political discussion of economic policy has drawn the interest of an ever-growing group of well-informed skeptics and policy opponents.[64] As a result, "civil servants and politicians alike have been increasingly obliged to seek an explicit rationale for their brand of economic knowledge."[65] Mary Furner and Barry Supple contend that "to the extent that economic efficiency or material well-being supersedes the other, perhaps even conflicting values, economic theory provides the best, conceivably the only, level at which a persuasive rationale for state policies can be found."[66] Ideas are causal beliefs that "derive authority from a shared consensus of recognized elites."[67]

Analytical foundations

We explain how ideas, as expressed through a paradigm change, influenced a neoliberal shift in two key areas of fiscal policy—deficit reduction and tax reform—through a series of analytic narratives focusing on the Reagan, Thatcher, Clinton, and Blair governments. By examining the influence of executive leaders within the context of a policy subsystem, we can account for the broader influence of interest groups, political parties, and other non-state actors in crafting major policy change.[68] This is particularly useful in helping us to identify linkages between changes in cognitive assumptions regarding economic problems and solutions and their effect on partisan convergence. For its many strengths, Peter Hall's model of paradigm change fails to specify adequately the "process" through which ideas become translated into concrete policies in a subsystem. At the same time, however, a focus purely on subsystems does not give us an adequate picture of the unique position of the executive in the agenda-setting and formulation process of fiscal policy. This is especially true when it comes to the executive's unique ability to initiate new policy trajectories from the "bully pulpit."

Coalitions within subsystems are forged by a common set of policy core beliefs that can include members of both partisan persuasions. In this process, the key figures on the Congressional Budget Committee and appropriation leaders in the House and Senate; think tanks; key journalists; and others play an important role in facilitating major shifts in policy over time. This is particularly true in the United States, where the separation of powers can produce a divided government. In the United States, one party may lead Congress and yet another may control the executive. As we see in Chapter 2, coalitions in a subsystem play a pivotal role in the British parliamentary system as well. Although they wield a significant amount of power in the arena of fiscal policy, executive leaders cannot afford to ignore broader subsystem influences.

Comparing partisan convergence in two pluralist democracies

The United States and Britain boast important similarities that render them ideal candidates for comparative analysis. Both countries possess a dominant two-party system, a pluralist political-economic system, and single-member plurality electoral districts. Sufficient congruity existent within the cases studied here helps to make our conclusions valid.

However, these cases were chosen as much for their differences as for their similarities. In analyzing the influence of shared ideas in the United States and Britain, it is important to recognize how different their economies are from each other. The United States has four times the population of Britain, and the level of real income per capita in the United States is almost 40 percent higher than in Britain.[69] International trade comprises less than 10 percent of the United States GNP as compared with 25 percent in Britain.[70] The United States, by way of comparison, is a relatively closed economy that presumably gives it much greater autonomy over its economic policy. Britain depends on world markets and, therefore, its domestic economy and economic policy are much more susceptible to external pressures.[71] Other important differences include the structure of economic policy making. The American political system is highly fragmented, given the nature of its separation of powers. Britain, by way of contrast, has a more centralized and hierarchical structure. Given these differences, it is very interesting "that events in the two countries in our period run parallel to the extent that they do."[72] These factors force us to highlight the influence of ideas on economic policy.

Why study tax policy and deficit reduction?

Taxation has been the central instrument of state economic policy since World War II and has long been at the center of the partisan conflict over the proper size, role, and functions of the modern state.[73] Tax systems in the United States and Britain "encompass a complex mix of competing goals, ambitions, and interests ... Raising revenue, redistributing income, encouraging savings, stimulating growth, penalizing consumption, directing investment, and rewarding certain values while penalizing others are just some of the hundreds of goals that any modern government tries to promote through its tax system."[74]

Chapters 3 and 4 seek to explain patterns of success and failure from the Reagan-Thatcher to the Clinton-Blair administrations. Sven Steinmo reveals that the United States and Britain now possess similar rates of corporate taxation. Patterns of change or continuity both within and among countries continue to be strongly influenced by endogenous factors. An ideas-based focus is useful in analyzing the transpartisan commitment to tax reform because it draws attention to several critical factors that have previously been ignored.

Despite much political rhetoric to the contrary, right- and left-of-center governments in both the United States and Great Britain were mutually responsible for the rise of the KWS and the associated increase in deficit spending. The economic conditions of the 1970s, however, served to support conservative charges that these uncontrollable deficit expenditures were driven, at least in part, by the ever-growing budgetary demands of the KWS. The idea that rising and apparently uncontrollable deficits could seriously damage a given nation's productivity began to be championed by moderates belonging to both the right and left of center. It was increasingly feared that massive debt financing would inevitably lead to an explosion of the money supply. Under these conditions, policy experts feared that both bond prices and exchange rates would plummet and domestic inflation would soar.

2 Paradigms, coalitions, and directional shifts in economic policy

This chapter examines the role of executive leaders and coalitions within policy subsystems in shaping major shifts in national economic policy in the United States and Britain. Executive leaders and coalitions in a subsystem are united by a shared set of core policy beliefs. Once a coalition successfully translates its beliefs into policy outcomes, a hegemonic policy paradigm may be established within the broader policy process. Timing is an important component of paradigm change, as the institution of new policy ideas will need to undergo a full policy cycle, which normally consists of formulation, implementation, and reformulation to allow the "enlightenment function" of policy research and experience to blossom. A decade or more is usually sufficient to test the usefulness of its causal assumptions and supply us with "a reasonably accurate portrait of program success and failure."[1]

Major changes in economic policy are ultimately shaped by participants who themselves are guided by a combination of empirical experience, social learning, and policy feedback. Policy actors are continuously learning about the policy environments in which they operate. They are constantly making evaluations about the usefulness of the strategies, theoretical assumptions, and techniques that are the base of the policy choices that they have made. Stated concisely, policy actors want to be assured that their policies "work" in the "real world" as they had initially predicted. If a set of major policies consistently fails to solve the problems that they were enacted to address, a search for alternatives will follow. Under such circumstances, contending groups of subsystem actors, whose policy views run counter to the dominant paradigm, will often use these conditions to advance their own ideas and policy strategies. This is particularly true in cases in which conditions are dire and conventional solutions have been exhausted.

Executive leaders, policy subsystems, and the importance of heresthetics

Successful executive leaders, and the subsystems of which they are a part, are defined by their ability to neutralize the opposition and build a political consensus around the coalition's core goals and beliefs.[2] The coalition must articulate clear alternatives to the existing policy within a coherent belief system or policy paradigm in a manner that is politically sustainable. This process is often facilitated by a major shift in the distribution of political and economic resources, such as money, votes, political capital invested by dominant coalitions and leaders, political commitments by dominant coalitions and leaders, and so on. These shifts are largely determined by events and activities external to the subsystem, such as a loss of political resources by a dominant group, or the successful strategies of their opponents may force actors in a subsystem to revise their policy beliefs.[3] In some cases, they may even incorporate aspects of their opponent's policy beliefs and strategies.[4]

As this book is confined to an analysis of the federal–national budgets in the United States and Britain, we take into account the influence of what Theodore Lowi terms "arenas of power."[5] Distinct institutional actors (e.g., the executive branch, the legislative branch, and the like) differ substantially in their ability to influence the policy agenda in different areas of public policy (e.g., regulatory, distributive, redistributive).[6] This by no means is meant to suggest that government institutions or agencies are monolithic. In fact, our treatment of the United States and Britain as pluralist democracies presumes the contrary. We simply contend that certain institutions may exercise greater influence in different areas of public policy. Institutions and formal rules provide relatively stable system parameters, which themselves are often altered during periods of major (third-order) policy change. Otherwise, however, institutional arrangements establish the basic parameters in which most routine political struggles take place. Most important, institutions and formal rules often determine who the key subsystem participants are.

Political institutions in the United States differ from those in Britain in several critical ways. It is important to lay out the formal structure of economic policy making in the United States and Britain, as this will provide the reader with important contextual insight related to the material presented in subsequent chapters. Table 2.1 provides an expanded list of subsystem actors involved in the US and British fiscal policy process.

The US fiscal policy subsystem

The structure of the economic policy system in the United States is relatively fragmented, given its separation of powers whereby the president and Congress may pursue distinct budgetary strategies. At the same time, political fragmentation extends within the executive branch itself. With the election of every new president, there is a considerable change in staff and personnel in the highest levels of the bureaucracy.[7] The Office of Management and Budget, under the oversight of its director, wields profound influence in creating and managing the overall budget. At the same time, the Council of

Table 2.1 Select list of important subsystem actors involved in the US and British fiscal policy processes

Select list of important subsystem actors involved in the US fiscal policy process

1 Office of the President
2 Council of Economic Advisors (Council of Economic Affairs—Reagan)
3 National Economic Council (Clinton)
4 Office of Management and Budget
5 Department of the Treasury (relevant offices and bureaus)
6 Congressional Budget Office (relevant departments)
7 House and Senate Appropriations Committees[1]
8 House Ways and Means and Senate Finance Committees[2]
9 The House and Senate Budget Committees[1]
10 Internal Revenue Service
11 Influential research institutes/think tanks
12 Key business groups
13 Interests groups (i.e., the American Tax Payers Association and Citizens for a Sound Economy)
14 Important journalists who frequently cover the issue

Select list of important subsystem actors involved in the fiscal policy process in Britain

1 Office of the Prime Minister/First Lord of the Treasury
2 Office of the Chancellor of the Exchequer
3 Chief Economic Advisor to the Treasury
4 Chief Secretary to the Treasury (deficit reduction)
5 The Department of Social Security
6 Paymaster-General
7 Financial Secretary to the Treasury
8 Economic Secretary to the Treasury
9 Spending ministers (deficit reduction)
10 Relevant cabinet committees
11 Business (Bank of England, Confederation of British Industry, Department of Trade and Industry)
12 Influential research institutes/think tanks with strong interest in economic policy
13 National Economic Development Council (NEDC) (until Thatcher)
14 Inland Revenue
15 Trades Union Congress (tax)
16 Important journalists who frequently cover the issue

Notes:
1 = deficit reduction; 2 = tax reform

Economic Advisors influences budgetary policy mainly through economic analysis for the president and is a key conduit for new economic ideas into the policy arena.[8]

Despite the enormous influence over the economic agenda that exists in the hands of the executive branch, affecting major economic policy change in tax reform and deficit reduction is a complex process that makes cooperation with the legislative branch particularly crucial. The passage of the Congressional Budget Impoundment and Control Act of 1974 represented the most important shift in the budget policy process since the Budget and Accounting Act of 1921.[9] The Act would augment Congress's power in the budget process without changing the president's role.[10] Changes stemming from the 1974 Act led to the creation of five distinct stages: (1) The president submits the budget he or she wants to Congress; (2) then Congress reviews the president's version and passes a budget resolution establishing spending and revenue limits; (3) after this stage, authorization bills are passed authorizing the expenditure of funds; (4) once Congress has authorized expenditures, appropriations bills are adopted to determine how and where the authorized expenditures will be spent; and finally (5), there is the reconciliation process that empowers the House and Senate budget committees to direct other committees to recommend actions that will bring policies and their costs within the overall spending limits as established by the budget resolutions.[11] Under the 1974 provisions, the budget committees could compel the legislative committees to amend the laws and, if necessary, force them to reconcile their recommendations with the overall budget resolution.[12] Throughout the 1980s and 1990s, the federal budget was most often presented in the form of the "Omnibus Reconciliation Acts."[13] When deficit targets began to be reached in the late 1990s under Clinton, the executive branch reasserted its dominance in the fiscal arena. In that process, the spending bills were separated once again, and the power held by the budget committees over the other spending committees was significantly reduced.

The White House and its Office of Management and Budget exercise enormous control over the policy agenda through its budget proposal to Congress. The White House's proposal informs Congress of the administration's budgetary goals regarding tax and spending initiatives.[14] However, Congress is able to exert considerable influence over how the nation's resources will be allocated to various federal programs. This is accomplished through House and Senate appropriations that deal with the amounts that will be spent on authorized programs.[15] The creation of the Congressional Budget Office and the standing House and Senate Budget Committees in the 1970s have provided the legislative branch with its own sources of policy expertise, enabling it to have a more influential role in the budgetary process. Balancing the budget, however, is not only the product of appropriations decisions but those regarding taxation as well.[16] Revenue decisions are the jurisdiction of both the House Ways and Means Committee and the Senate Finance Committee.[17] The budget committees are also important conduits in this process. They are responsible for drafting the budget resolutions that outline targets for the forthcoming fiscal year for revenues, total spending, and the thirteen appropriations bills. The budget committees must then persuade the tax and appropriations committees to adopt them.[18]

Despite the growing influence of the Congress in tax reform and deficit reduction matters, the executive branch remains preeminent in setting the budgetary agenda. Initially, the introduction of neoliberal ideas into the advisory process occurred under the Reagan administration; however, these ideas continued to be massively influential in shaping the policy goals of the Clinton administration. This shift in economic policy goals was driven by a combination of economic expertise and electoral politics. It was "the culmination of a long process of grass-roots political agitation and organization which formed the ideological background of the 'Counter Establishment' in the USA."[19] The movement included an intellectual coalition of neoliberal advocates from research institutes and think tanks (e.g., American Enterprise Institute, The Brookings Institute, the Cato Institute, the Heritage Foundation, and the like) who coalesced with key actors from the elite media and certain business groups.[20] In the same way, the neoliberal orientation of the Clinton administration can be linked to its involvement with the Democratic Leadership Council (DLC) and the Progressive Policy Institute. The DLC and the Progressive Policy Institute were both established by neoliberal Democrats who embraced the logic of fiscal prudence and individual responsibility. Members belonging to these organizations jointly advocated the market mechanism for allocating society's resources wherever possible. A shared core belief in the supremacy of individual responsibility and private initiative in creating societal wealth brought DLC activists together. These beliefs ran counter to the KWS and its core assumptions regarding the positive relationship between government-led redistribution and economic growth. In adopting these beliefs, these "new Democrats" had embraced critical elements of traditional conservatism and monetarism.

British fiscal policy subsystem

Prior to the 1960s, the budgetary process in Britain proceeded in a rather informal and often unsystematic manner. The process changed dramatically in the wake of the economic shocks of the 1970s when the British established the Public Expenditure Survey Committee, making it more formalized, systematic, and procedure-driven. In the first stage of the process, three-year budget estimates are submitted by the spending ministers who head the various governmental departments to the Chief Secretary of the Treasury and then later to the Cabinet at large, which then assesses the spending needs for the next five years. The next stage involves intense bilateral negotiations between the Treasury ministers and the spending department ministers over spending limits and priorities. The large spending departments, such as Health and Social Security, Defence, and Education, serve powerful constituencies that compel them to seek increasing amounts of funding, while Treasury ministers are pressured to balance the various needs of the different spending departments within the confines of a limited budget. Budget compromises that result from these proceedings are submitted to the Cabinet committees that deal with specific policy areas before being submitted to the full Cabinet for approval. If not satisfied with the outcome, spending ministers may appeal to the Star Chamber that is composed of senior Cabinet ministers whose purpose is to settle disagreements between spending and Treasury ministers.

Although the structure of economic policy making in Britain is generally much more centralized than that in the United States, Prime Ministers and their Cabinets also rely on the political support within policy subsystems in bringing about third-order policy change. The fiscal policy process in Britain is far more deliberative and inclusive than is often presumed. In very recent years, the British economic policy structure has become increasingly decentralized. Such government agencies as the Department of Social Security, the Home Office, and the Department for Employment and Education, have become important actors in the economic policy arena, once almost entirely dominated by the Treasury and the Department of Trade and Industry.[21] Blair's quest to replace traditional unemployment welfare with "workfare" has greatly increased the involvement of these and other department actors in shaping the budget policy process.

Spending, and hence deficit reduction, is an especially politicized area of economic policy wherein the broader influence of coalition actors can ill afford to be ignored. As we examine more carefully in Chapter 3, the deficit reduction efforts undertaken in the Reagan and Thatcher eras became inextricably linked with cuts in public spending. Nigel Lawson, Chancellor of the Exchequer (1984–8), concedes that "curbing the growth of public spending is one of the hardest tasks facing any government since it affects services which people have come to consider as rights and [thus] involves taking on powerful public sector lobbies."[22] Given this fact, it is clear that the influence of public sector lobbies and other subsystem actors must be taken into account when analyzing the politics of spending cuts and deficit reduction in Britain.

Examining British tax reform at the subsystem level is also both appropriate and useful. Generally speaking, revenue decisions or taxation have not been as susceptible to the influence of broader subsystem pressures. Nevertheless, a number of developments that have occurred have rendered revenue decisions less impervious to influences in the broader policy subsystem. Important pieces of evidence are offered in support of this claim. When the medium-term financial strategy was introduced in 1979 by the new Thatcher government, its main effect was to bring tax and spending policy together in the name of fiscal stability. The Thatcher government's "wholesale switch from an income to an expenditure tax system" was designed largely in accordance with specific recommendations originally proposed in the Meade Report of 1976 and developed in consultation with officials in the Inland Revenue.[23] Further, Claudio M. Radaelli asserts that think tanks, such as the Institute of Economic Affairs, have "had a remarkable track record on individual income taxation."[24] Whereas Nigel Lawson vehemently rejected recommendations from the Institute of Fiscal Studies to adopt a preliminary or green budget, in a conciliatory move, the Chancellor released green papers covering a number of critical tax reform initiatives (save the corporate tax reform of 1984).[25] The development of regular pre-budget reports, introduced under the Blair government, has made the budgetary process increasingly deliberative. Most importantly, however, is the resiliency of the ideas themselves governing tax reform and deficit reduction. There has been remarkable consistency in fiscal policy ideas and goals adopted by right-of-center governments under Margaret Thatcher and John Major to the left-of-center government led by Tony Blair. Cabinets and ministers have come and gone over the past 20 years, but neoliberal changes in tax policy goals and strategies have, in a broad sense, proceeded with remarkable consistency. The congruity of policy subsystems and the policy beliefs they advocate are an integral factor in explaining policy change over time.

Think tanks, elite journalists, and other critical subsystem actors were instrumental in bringing about neoliberal economic policy change during the Thatcher era.[26] The shift began as economic stagflation ensued and the Keynesian consensus began to unravel. In this process, declining economic conditions provided the opportunity for anti-Keynesian think tanks (e.g., the Centre for Policy Studies and the Institute of Economic Affairs) that were organized around neoliberal principles to enter and ultimately dominate the policy discourse.[27] The neoliberal agenda was further supported by the Adam Smith Institute that is intellectually aligned with the ideas of Fredrich Von Hayek and the Austrian school of economics, in conjunction with the Institute of Directors, which adopted a traditional (as opposed to Laffer-curve) supply-side approach.[28] These research institutes were organized within a broader network that included critical business interests, such as the Confederation of British Industry, such important elite journalists as Samuel Brittan of the *Financial Times*, and independent economists who provided political support and economic advice for Thatcher's neoliberal agenda.[29] According to Otto Singer, the prime minister "could and did rely heavily on experts from the anti-Keynesian network of economists."[30] Thatcher formally introduced this group of influential "outside" advisers into the policy process in the form of the Prime Minister's Policy Unit.[31]

During the Thatcher–Major era, major reforms took place in the structure of the public service sector. Most notable, and counter-intuitive, was the growth in both influence and number of quasi-autonomous nongovernmental organizations, or "quangos." According to the Democratic Audit conducted in 1994, there were more than 6,700 quangos, of which more than 5,500 had executive power, operating in a variety of policy subsystems throughout the country.[32] These organizations have been performing public service functions outlined, but not directly controlled, by the government. Although quasi-autonomous, quangos are financed by the government, and their directors and managing committees are usually nominated by officials in Whitehall.

Quangos and extra-governmental organizations serve a variety of functions and operate at various stages of the public policy process. They may be heavily involved in implementing policy or merely serve as advisory bodies in policy formulation. They exist in most areas of social and economic policy and are often created in response to pressures from such interest groups as business organizations or labor unions. Quangos themselves fall into several sets of categories. The first are nondepartmental public bodies. These include regulatory bodies concerning such areas as public utilities, the arts council, and the Commission for Racial Equality. Other organizations and agencies under this category include the BBC in the area of broadcasting; the Manpower Services Commission and the Training and Education Councils in the area of labor market policy; housing action trusts; and hospitals and family health services in the area of social policy.[33] The next category consists of advisory nondepartmental public bodies that include various governmental and parliamentary commissions.[34] Another set of quangos includes tribunals that serve judicial functions, such as the benefit appeals tribunals.[35] The final category includes the National Health Service administrative bodies.[36] The increase in the number of quangos since the Thatcher–Major era has significantly shaped the public policy landscape in Britain. For example, the neoliberal push toward the privatization of the major public utilities led to the creation of regulatory agencies, such as Oftel, Ofgas, and Ofwat, to monitor pricing and quality in the areas of telephone services, gas, and water supplies. Quangos have become critical subsystem players in influencing the substance and direction of fiscal policy.

Under the leadership of Tony Blair, an expert advisory system has emerged as a vital component in shaping economic policy outcomes. Under Blair, neoliberal ideas have been formally institutionalized within the internal advisory system of the Treasury itself. The Blair government sought to build greater coordination among the various policy networks in the economic subsystem. The Prime Minister, the Chancellor of the Exchequer, the Chief Secretary, and the other important economic ministers (including the Paymaster-General, the Financial Secretary to the Treasury, the Economic Secretary to the Treasury, and their special advisers) share a resolute commitment to both fiscal discipline and transparency in economic policy consistent with neoliberal directives. In addition, the Blair government has relied on the expert policy analysis of a group of special advisers in the Treasury. "Labour's faceless wonders" as christened by John Prescott, the Deputy Prime Minister, have played a critical role in the development and implementation of neoliberalism-oriented policy strategies from welfare-to-work to business tax reform in contemporary Britain. Most of the 68 members in this group, whose average age is 36 (only four of whom are older than 50), share highly similar neoliberal views on the economy.[37] According to *The Times*, "sixteen are journalists; seven worked in lobbying or public relations; six have been think tank researchers. And unthinkable in the party 10 years ago, there are only four trade unionists."[38] The majority of the special advisement team members attended state schools, but more than one-third attended either Oxford or Cambridge.[39]

Since the late 1990s, the policy advisory system in Whitehall has been focused on the proposition that fiscal policy must be both prudent and predictable in order to encourage the accumulation of new capital investment now deemed necessary to secure long-term growth. The instrument that "institutionalized" this core belief is the Code for Fiscal Stability. The Code, which was adopted in the 1998 budget, lays out explicit guidelines that must be included in the government's fiscal agenda.[40] From the very beginning, particular emphasis was placed on the area of debt management. Most important, the Code made the budgetary process in Britain significantly more deliberative in nature. In seeking to bring greater transparency to the policy-making process, the Treasury now publishes a pre-budget report, or green budget, that has opened the budgetary process and key elements of proposed tax and spending issues to debate and criticism. The Code has further introduced specific limits on government borrowing for public investment and disallows its use for funding of current expenditure.[41] It mandates that policy must "take account of risk and of need, so far as possible, to avoid conflict with monetary policy."[42]

The Blair government's political commitment to fiscal discipline provides a powerful vindication of the neoliberal paradigm in Britain. The adoption of the provisions set forth in the Code for Fiscal Stability provide compelling evidence to support the assertion that neoliberal ideas have, at long last, been institutionalized in the formal budget policy-making process.[43] The most compelling example of this point, however, comes in the form of the Blair government's decision to grant the Bank of England monetary autonomy in setting short-term interest rates. In successfully bringing about central bank independence, the Blair government has demonstrated its formal commitment to neoliberal fiscal goals.

Role of policy subsystems and policy paradigms in explaining the decline of the KWS paradigm

Role of discourse in policy change and continuity

Policy discourse lies at the root of policy paradigms. This study relies on the analysis of externally driven change as a necessary component for explaining major shifts in a given policy discourse. Discourse "refers to a subjective framing of an issue which helps those who participate in debate define themselves in terms of it; and it helps to define the terms of the debate, in particular, the conceptual vocabulary, material referents, and the stakes involved."[44] It further concerns "the interactions of individuals, interest groups, social movements, and institutions through which problematic situations are converted to policy problems, agendas are set, decisions are made, and actions are taken."[45]

When discourse takes place in the public arena, it does so within particular forums or institutional venues for policy debate.[46] As this study analyzes the role of discourse within the context of formal politics, it is appropriate to conceive of it as contributing to the "ongoing struggle among political parties."[47] Therefore, "disputes within a discourse have to do with the struggle for standing [wherein] those presently excluded from the conversation strive to get in."[48] A fundamental part of this struggle is driven by politico-economic groups seeking to institutionalize a particular set of ideas through state action.[49] It is important to understand that coalitional actors within a sub-system seek to shape the policy debate within specific dimensions, rendering a major shift in the existing policy discourse an unusual and phenomenal event occurring only under extraordinary circumstances.

The role of anomalies

An anomaly is a phenomenon that is not anticipated or cannot be explained by the reigning paradigm. Over time, the accretion of anomalies can cause policy actors to make amendments to the dominant paradigm or, in some extraordinary circumstances, replace it altogether. John F. Munro contends that "only when there has been a fundamental, unmistakable failure in the policy paradigm will policymakers consider altering normative and onto-logical axioms."[50] Where the accumulation of anomalies is sufficient to constitute a crisis, a new paradigm may eventually dominate the policy discourse if it can be shown to be a viable alternative.

Anomalies, which are "mistaken forecasts" of real-world phenomena, are critical factors in causing policy communities to adopt drastically altered interpretations of how the economy functions.[51] Neo-Keynesian policies in the United States and Britain were based on the Phillips curve–assumption of a tradeoff between inflation and unemployment.[52] Beginning in the late 1960s, a major anomaly emerged in the economies of the United States and Britain that the Keyensian paradigm failed to address adequately. Traditional "demand-managed" remedies seemed to have a negligible effect in bringing down inflation and unemployment that, by the mid-1970s, had reached crisis proportions. In fact, they were ultimately seen by policy experts to be a contributory cause of economic stagnation and unemployment.[53] In light of these anomalies, policy makers began considering alternative economic policy ideas and strategies.[54]

The role that crises play

A crisis is a cataclysmic event (e.g., war, depression, and the like) that causes enormous suffering or uncertainty (or both) among groups and individuals within the state as well as the society.[55] In conditions of crisis, "orthodox" policy strategies are called into question for their ability adequately to resolve new and often unforeseen economic problems.[56] In periods of crisis, information disseminated and received by participants is often imprecise and insufficient for them to make rational decisions. In cases in which information is asymmetrically shared by participants, traditional coalitions (e.g., the New Deal in the United States and Beveridge in Britain) that were built and maintained by the logic and stability of the preexisting paradigm become highly susceptible to divisive pressures. Under such conditions, existing coalitions are likely to unravel or become reorganized around a new set of ideas and policy agendas.

Participants need to have some means of identifying and evaluating a crisis before they can begin to mobilize the necessary political and economic resources for dealing with it. This is important because "a crisis diagnosis makes a strong explanatory claim" about the appropriateness of selecting a desired set of means to attain desired ends.[57] Crises often open the policy dialog to new participants and points of view. "Suffering often inspires the search for new and radical solutions, giving rise to a higher-level image of the world which brings old and new experiences into an intelligible and coherent relation."[58]

The effects of economic stagflation that occurred in the mid-1970s in both the United States and Britain demonstrate a case wherein a major crisis dramatically challenged fundamental assumptions of how the economy functioned. Clark, Stewart, and Zuk provide a succinct account of the events that led to the crisis and how the two countries reacted:

> Although the extent of the economic downturn varied from one country to the next, the patterns were broadly similar—sharp increases in inflation and unemployment and sluggish growth became the new defining characteristics of Western economies ... In Britain, joblessness followed a steadily upward course for much of the decade. In the United States, although the pattern was more variable, average levels of unemployment were also high and occasional downward movements were modest and short-lived.[59]

During this period, dramatic contradictions became highly apparent as the economies in both countries behaved in ways that could not be explained by the reigning paradigm. The "zero-sum economic conditions of the 1970s" imposed a formidable strain on the historic New Deal and Beveridge compromises that had been forged in the 1930s and 1940s.[60] Economic interests became increasingly polarized and competitive in the face of increasingly scarce resources.[61] In the previous era, an enduring period of sustained private-sector growth enabled supporters of the KWS to maintain and expand ambitious (redistributive) social programs. With the advent of the energy and international monetary crises and with declining industrial growth in the 1970s, however, policy makers were faced with acute distributive dilemmas that began to undermine the ideational foundations on which the KWS consensus was based.[62] The main target of attack was the redistributive social agenda that it spawned. In the malaise of slow growth and high inflation that came to characterize the US and British economies in the mid-1970s, a growing number of neoliberal critics asserted that the two countries could no longer afford the redistributive programs that had been developed and expanded in the KWS era. By the late 1970s, policy solutions calling for the redistribution of income from government to the private sector and from consumption to saving and productive investment were gaining increased salience among the policy elite belonging to both the left and right of center in the United States and Britain.

Role of learning

Jack Levy defines experimental learning as "a change of beliefs (or the degree of confidence in a certain set of beliefs) or the development of new beliefs, skills, or procedures as a result of the observation and interpretation of experience."[63] Policy learning is the continuous process of exploration and experimentation with policy alternatives that is driven by the desire to realize core policy beliefs.[64] Fundamental change in a coalition's belief system requires the gradual accumulation of evidence over time, although this is not sufficient to cause a change in the core aspects of public policy.[65] Rather, such change also requires an external shock that occurs outside the policy subsystem, perhaps in the form of a cataclysmic event that subsequently results in fundamentally altering the current allocation of political resources.[66] External shocks, or anomalies, that occur from outside the policy community, are the pivotal factor in bringing about a major shift in policy paradigms. Under such conditions, "the political resources of minority coalitions in the policy-making process can be markedly increased," providing it with ample strength to redesign policy goals in a manner that is consistent with their beliefs.[67]

The recession of the 1970s illuminates this point. Initially, there was much disagreement on how to cope with the crisis. Clarke, Stewart, and Zuk give a concise account of the dimensions of the policy debate that developed in response to the crisis:

> One response was simply business as usual, that is, attempts to employ standard Keynesian demand-management techniques to control inflation and unemployment to stimulate economic growth. A second response involved the development of administrative procedures to control the costs of increasingly expensive welfare programs by eliminating waste and mismanagement and by strictly enforcing program eligibility requirements.[68]

The paradigm that resulted from the intellectual assault on the KWS and the logic that underpinned the redistributive policy structure comprised "a more consistent assertion of the neoclassical paradigm."[69] At the same time, additional economic problems that developed in the 1970s provided a catalyst for policymakers to shift their attention to the supply side of the economy.[70] Both the US and British economies simultaneously experienced large decreases in GDP after the first oil shock. The effects of slow growth were especially pronounced in the areas of capital formation and productivity, which had fallen dramatically by the mid-1970s.[71] As these conditions worsened and traditional demand-side policies failed to provide the solutions that policymakers expected, new ideas began to gain appeal in the policy discourse.

Shift from Keynesianism to neoliberalism

Neoliberalism began emerging in the United States as a salient alternative to the KWS in the early 1970s. Conservative thinkers, such as Irving Kristol, realized that the intellectual foundation for "progressive" social policy, which rested at the base of the KWS, was critically supported by Keynes-oriented think tanks. Kristol believed that the most effective way to create conservative change was through the establishment of conservatively oriented think tanks to counter the influence of Keynesian hegemony in the policy discourse.[72] The point was well received among business executives who were growing disenchanted with the current direction of economic policy. According to David Stoesz, "Chief executive officers of America's major corporations responded with a vengeance, writing checks directly, or diverting funds indirectly through foundations, to a new intellectual infrastructure of neoliberal policy institutes."[73]

In this environment, conservative think tanks, such as the American Enterprise Institute (AEI) and the Heritage Foundation flourished. Stoesz brings out that "by the time of the 1980 election, AEI had 30 scholars and fellows in residence, 77 adjunct scholars, and 250 professors associated with the institute nationwide. AEI's staff and board members represented a who's who of the nation's business and political elite."[74] During the reign of the Reagan administration, the Heritage Foundation had more than 35 staff in upper-level positions in the executive branch. By the mid-1980s, like think tanks as AEI, Heritage, Cato, and Hoover had become instrumental in initiating the neoliberal paradigm shift in the United States. These groups shared broadly similar views on the need for greater privatization, lower taxes, and reducing the size of the deficit.

Over time, these "new" conservative economic ideas began to transcend partisan lines. Neoliberalism, as it came to be called, began gaining appeal among centrists and conservatives in the Democratic Party as well. According to David Stoesz, with the massive defeat of Walter Mondale by Ronald Reagan in 1984, the leaders in the Democratic Party were forced fundamentally to reexamine the party's existing ideas and raison d'état. The Democratic Party's leadership and policy base was again severely shaken in 1988 when Michael Dukakis lost the presidential election while the federal budget deficit continued to soar under George H. Bush.[75] In the midst of these electoral defeats, which were viewed by many as larger indictments of the continued relevance of the Democratic Party's policy ideas for the modern era, a small of group neoliberal Democrats began to create an alliance within the party in an attempt to move it to the right on economic issues.

The impetus for a major ideational shift within the Democratic Party was the acceptance that neo-Keynesian ideas no longer provided useful and appropriate remedies.[76] The declining significance of Keynesian-led fiscal policy encouraged several moderate Democrats such as Bill Clinton and Al Gore to support the formation of the Democratic Leadership Council, that was established in 1985, in an effort to bring neoliberal thought into the Party's mainstream.[77] Guided by their admiration of the remarkable success that conservative think tanks enjoyed in supporting Reagan's neoliberal agenda, centrists in the DLC built an intellectual alliance with the Progressive Policy Institute headed by Will Marshall in an effort to advance their own neoliberal agenda. This group embraced a commitment to the need to restrain unfocused spending and waste that had become associated with big-government liberalism.[78] The DLC asserted that there was a direct causal link between the long-term solvency of Social Security and the socioeconomic health of the economy. To ensure the latter, the DLC argued that the country needed to adopt a rigorous commitment to high-skills job creation and deficit reduction.[79] With the election of Bill Clinton and Al Gore in 1992, moderates had taken a major step forward toward establishing neoliberalism as the hegemonic paradigm in the policy discourse.

The question now was how successful moderate Democrats would be in translating these beliefs into tangible policy outcomes. David Stoesz brings out that:

> In no time the new paradigm thesis was central to contemporary political analysis. David Osborne teamed up with Ted Gaebler to write "Reinventing Government," a manifesto on revitalizing local governance that called for a new generation of solutions … The director of the Progressive Policy Institute, Will Marshall exploited the ideological opening stating that "the dominant ideas of both parties had outlived their time," and offered a new social contract in their stead. Following his election to the Presidency, Bill Clinton put the new paradigm to use in outlining his economic program.[80]

In the later years of its first term and continuing through its second, the Clinton administration found the proposition of a balanced budget to be realistic and one that a majority in Congress would now support rather than hinder. Members on both sides of the political fence in the legislature had warmed to the notion that balancing the budget should be the most important goal on the fiscal agenda. This group of neoliberals held the belief that any tax reforms would have to be designed in accordance with deficit reduction goals as the primary focus. By 1998, the Clinton administration and critical legislative actors had successfully forged a bipartisan coalition that was able, at long last, to present a balanced budget. Chapter 4 explains in greater detail how the change in partisan leadership in Congress in 1994 was instrumental in facilitating this milestone achievement.

Having presided over a robust economy that boasted relatively low inflation and a budget surplus, the Clinton administration and key members in Congress turned their attention to the issue of tax reform. Arguments over the appropriate size of the tax cuts themselves, however, would continue to divide ardent tax cutters in Congress, such as House Ways and Means Committee chairman William Archer (R-TX) and Majority Leader Dick Armey (R-TX), against the administration and other deficit cutters in Congress. Although they were committed to the proposition of using at least part of the budget surplus to finance a series of important tax cuts rather than new spending, the Clinton administration and its bipartisan coalition partners in Congress, such as Senate Budget Committee chairman Pete Domenici (R-NM) and House Budget Committee chairman John R. Kasich (R-OH), proceeded with extreme caution. Their first concern was guaranteeing the solvency of both Social Security and Medicare.

Much as in the United States, Keynesian directives for dealing with economic adjustment in Britain were discredited in the crisis that ensued in the 1970s. According to Otto Singer, "the decisive turning point in British economic policy was the election of Margaret Thatcher. The combination of [classic] economic liberalism and monetarism, which was at the heart of the post-1979 British economic policy broke with the past."[81] By the early 1980s, the paradigm guiding economic policy in the Treasury shifted decisively from the KWS toward monetarism.[82] The shift was largely facilitated by the Prime Minister's appointment of monetarists to key positions in the Treasury.[83] Specifically, the medium-term financial strategy, the thrust of the Thatcher government's fiscal reform agenda, arose from proposals by Alan Budd, Terry Burns, and Tim Congdon.[84]

The developments described here created a hospitable policy environment for a new brand of ideas and research institutes that effectively challenged the reigning orthodoxy. The Centre for Policy Studies, established jointly by Sir Keith Joseph and Margaret Thatcher, was the intellectual hub of the monetarist policy apparatus.[85] The Centre became a focal point for the emerging school of monetarism, which underpinned the conservative manifesto for the 1979 general election and the course of fiscal policy that would be pursued by the Conservative government. In the same way, the

Institute of Economic Affairs, the Adam Smith Institute, and the Institute of Directors, played a pivotal role in introducing Milton Friedman-style monetarism into the political and intellectual discourse.[86] Such economists as Patrick Minford, Alan Walters, Alan Budd, Terry Burns, and Michael Laidler became leading advocates of monetarist ideas in the policy arena. Elite journalists, such as William Rees-Mogg, Samuel Brittan, Bernard Levin, and Peter Jay of the *Times*, along with Ronald Butt at the *Sunday Times*, helped to mobilize broad support outside the state that "virtually forced the Whitehall machine to alter its mode of macroeconomic policymaking."[87]

Much like the Reagan experience, support for the new paradigm went broadly unfulfilled. In the final analysis, the broader Tory membership in Britain proved unwilling or unable to support Thatcher's austere fiscal program and the "traditional left" seemed unwilling at that time to begin any serious reexamination of the KWS paradigm. This left the completion of the neoliberal agenda and, more precisely, the program of fiscal austerity in the hands of Tony Blair and the modernizers in the Labour party. The Blair government took a very aggressive and decisive move toward institutionalizing critical components of monetarism, focusing first and foremost on stabilizing the money supply, placing this cause ahead of the goal of full employment. At the same time, the leftist government adopted critical elements of traditional conservatism by focusing on the private sector of the economy in expanding economic growth.

The creation of the special advisers unit was a key component in carrying through neoliberal change. Whitehall's monetarist-traditional conservative alliance with the intellectual elite is most visible through its connection with the London School of Economics. This alliance can be directly traced from Downing Street to the school's current director, Anthony Giddens, who is well known for both his support of the Blair government and his extensive writings on the "third-way" economic agenda. The Blair government established an intellectual alliance early on with the "non-partisan" Demos Institute and the Institute for Public Policy Research. In fact, the cofounder of Demos, Geoff Mulgan, later served in "Number 10" as the leader of Downing Street's Social Exclusion Unit. Finally, the Commission on Social Justice, established by the Institute for Public Policy Research, was instrumental in redefining the aims of the "new Labour" party and its view of the role of the state in modern society.[88] Specifically, the Commission's report asserted that state's role in the economy should be "enabling rather than paternalistic."[89] This view represented a significant departure from the party's previous view of the role of the state in society. For example, supporters of the Commission asserted that the legitimate role of the state is to help individuals to move from welfare to work, to establish a fair and investment-driven taxation system, and to help workers to update trade skills through a strategy of life-long learning.[90] The Commission held that individuals have a corresponding responsibility to "work where work is available" and designed these strategies in accordance with the belief that the state could no longer sustain traditional welfare collectivism or seek full employment by expanding the public sector.[91] The state, once viewed as "a guarantor of social rights of relatively passive social actors," is now seen as "an enabler and supporter of active individuals ..."[92]

3 Deficit reduction and tax reform in the Reagan–Thatcher era

Neoliberal tax reform and deficit reduction reforms initiated under Reagan and Thatcher are compared in this chapter. An examination of the period from 1979 to 1991 has led us to three main conclusions. First, distinct fiscal strategies pursued by the Reagan and Thatcher administrations reflect differences in their core and secondary policy beliefs. Second, although Thatcher demonstrated a stronger commitment to deficit reduction than did Reagan, both leaders suffered major defeats in realizing their original fiscal goals. In the final analysis, both Reagan and Thatcher could not muster sufficient political support to institute the spending cuts that were required to eliminate the fiscal deficit within their respective countries. In this chapter, we analyze the deficit reduction and tax reform initiatives under the Reagan and Thatcher governments by focusing on ideas and coalitions in explaining patterns of policy success and failure. Third, despite the policy setbacks that Reagan and Thatcher experienced in the 1980s, their pioneering experiments with neoliberalism-oriented spending and tax reforms in that era laid the critical foundation for the fiscal policy course that was later pursued and consolidated by successive governments of the left in the 1990s.

Deficit reduction in the United States and Britain

By the end of the 1970s, deficit spending in both the United States and Britain had become an ineluctable characteristic of the Keynesian welfare state (KWS) policy apparatus. This was due to the fact that the maintenance and continued growth of public spending for politically desirable, but often very expensive, social policies eventually led to undesired economic conditions, wherein spending dramatically exceeded receipts collected by the state from tax revenues. In the United States, for example, deficit spending began approaching $150 billion during the 1980s and eventually climbed to nearly $300 billion by 1992.[1] In the same way, the deficit reached as high as £50 billion in Britain in the early 1990s.

This chapter explores the factors that contributed to the failure of Reagan's and Thatcher's balanced budget agendas in the 1980s. With at least two explanations that address this issue we have the most sympathy. The first has to do with the issue of institutional fragmentation and the specter of divided government in the United States. Scholars who pose this argument assert that Reagan's inability to balance the budget was due mostly to the fact that the Democrat-controlled Congress blocked the initiatives of the Republican administration in its attempts to control fiscal expenditure. This explanation, however, fails to account for the fact that Thatcher, who presided over a unitary system, also experienced comparable setbacks and disappointments. Given the concentration of political authority that resides in the British Treasury, the Thatcher government should have been well positioned for instituting the large spending cuts deemed necessary for eliminating the deficit. As it turns out, Reagan and Thatcher actually encountered the same problem, although for different reasons. In the end, both leaders faced what Paul Pierson and R. Kent Weaver have each termed "the politics of blame avoidance."[2] Whereas the Reagan administration was constrained by the separation of powers, Thatcher was constrained by what Pierson calls the "concentration of accountability."[3] Therefore, institutional differences seem to cancel each other out.

The second explanation posits that the recession of the early 1980s (and the drop in expected revenues that followed) severely jeopardized any serious deficit reduction effort. However, although it is certainly true that the recession contributed significantly to a major reduction in receipts, this does not account for the fact that the United States and Britain continued to run enormous deficits well after their economies recovered. Economic recoveries in the United States and Britain, after all, should have led to a substantial reduction in the deficit in both countries but, instead, both countries continued to run increasingly high deficits.[4]

Deficit as a salient issue in the United States and Britain

Since the Reagan–Thatcher era, deficit reduction has become a salient political issue in both the United States and Britain. This phenomenon has been driven by at least two developments. First, officials in both the United States and Britain have grown increasingly sensitive to the effect of deficit spending on the overall public debt in these countries.[5] In FY 1999, for example, it was forecast that the US government would spend 14 percent of its budget to service the interest on the debt for that fiscal year. In the same way, public concern over deficit spending reached its peak in Britain in the mid-1990s when taxpayers became aware that the government was spending more on the interest on the national debt than on the country's entire public education system.[6] Although public attention over the deficit reached its zenith in the 1990s, a group of *deficit hawks* began raising red flags as to its dangers as far back as the 1970s. These deficit hawks were composed of a small but cohesive group of politicians, economic experts, and business organizations in both countries that began drawing attention to the potential economic dangers associated with accruing large levels of public debt.[7] Deficit hawks in both countries argued that deficit spending and consequent increases in the public debt were crippling the US and British private economies. Second, by the mid-1980s, national-level economic policy makers in both the United States and Britain had widely accepted the notion that promoting economic growth meant adopting policies that were aimed first and foremost at encouraging greater private investment. It became increasingly believed by critical groups of policy makers in both countries that excessive levels of public borrowing "crowded out" potential capital available for private investment.

These "new" policy beliefs were embedded in neoliberal economic principles. The neoliberal paradigm represented a fundamentally different set of axioms regarding how the economy worked from that of the KWS. Whereas the KWS was built on the premise that it was possible for governments to predict and adjust for market failure, neoliberalism shifted public awareness to the propensity to government failure. Specifically, neoliberals (composed of Laffer-curve supply-siders), traditional conservatives, and monetarists were aligned in their general criticism of government intervention in the market place. The Reagan administration offered sharp criticism of government's capacity for "waste, fraud, extravagance, and abuse."[8] According to William Niskanen, "The new Reagan administration recognized that the President's overall economic plan could not succeed without a sharp reduction in the spending growth trend built into current law and policy."[9]

The essence of the neoliberal movement that Reagan and Thatcher led was directed fundamentally at dismantling the redistributive policy apparatus. Reaganomics entailed a perplexing paradox with respect to deficit reduction. On the one hand, Reagan's continuous and systematic rhetorical assaults on the welfare state and big government opened the fiscal-policy window in a manner that enabled deficit cutters to promote their cause to a higher status on the policy agenda. On the other hand, Reagan's contradictory economic strategies led to unintended massive increases in the budget deficit in the immediate years of his administration. By 1982, economic officials in the United States increasingly began to regard enormous deficit spending and resulting increases in public debt as a major problem that would ultimately lead to a full-blown crisis if left unattended.[10]

Beginning in 1981 and 1982, the United States began experiencing between receipts and outlays enormous disparities that by the end of the decade culminated into a fiscal catastrophe. Those fateful first budgets of the Reagan administration set US fiscal policy on a runaway course of deficit spending that would take nearly a decade and a half to end. In evaluating why deficit spending has generated so much concern in the economic policy discourse in recent times, one cannot ignore the pivotal role of policy learning through feedback from experience. Policy makers in both the United States and Britain were compelled to rethink their support of the KWS, and the notion of big government inspired remedies that had led to ever-growing levels of public expenditure and huge structural deficits. Many policy makers adjusted their positions in light of a growing body of empirical evidence regarding the national deficit and its effect on real and potential private investment and economic growth. According to Michael Boskin, by the mid-1980s, policy-makers in the United States were becoming increasingly receptive to empirical findings "that deficits contribute to high interest rates, both directly through government borrowing in credit markets, and indirectly through uncertainty over their likely economic effects."[11] By the early 1990s, budget deficits in the United States had risen to nearly $300 billion a year.

In Britain, the deficit rose steadily in the 1970s owing to a combination of expansionist policies enacted by the Heath government in conjunction with the recession and rise in inflation in 1974 and 1975.[12] Nigel Lawson revealed that by the 1980s, Thatcher and her core supporters viewed the deficit to be a direct threat to the financial well-being of Britain.[13] In his address to the *Financial Times* Euromarkets Conference in 1980, Lawson asserted that "too high a PSBR [public sector borrowing requirement] requires either that the government borrows heavily from the banks, which adds directly to the money supply; or failing this, that it borrows from individuals and institutions, but at ever increasing rates of interest which place an unacceptable squeeze on the private sector."[14]

Deficit reduction in the Reagan era

In 1981, President Reagan embarked on a neoliberal course to dismantle the KWS that had reigned as the hegemonic paradigm since the 1930s and 1940s. However, he sought what even many conservative critics charged were mutually unobtainable objectives: to cut taxes, accelerate the defense buildup, restrain domestic spending, and balance the budget. In pursuing what these critics viewed as competing (if not contradictory) objectives, the Reagan administration found itself unable to break the pattern whereby federal spending continued to increase as a percentage of GNP. Nevertheless, Reagan's assaults on overall public spending led to a slowdown in the rate of increase of government outlays "substantially from what it had been during the Carter era (from an inflation-adjusted real growth rate of about 44 percent to 33 percent in Reagan's first term in office, then to about 18 percent during his second term)."[15]

In bringing about these rather modest cuts in the rate of increase in government expenditure, the Reagan administration sought to sever one of the main arteries of the KWS. The administration's attention to the deficit reduction issue helped to promote the neoliberal paradigm within the fiscal policy discourse. Through its continuous rhetorical assaults on increased social spending, the administration effectively began to prime the policy discourse for the ascension of conservative and monetarist economic principles regarding the importance of fiscal discipline. Most importantly, however, these ideas laid the foundation for the deficit reduction agenda that would be championed by the Clinton administration almost a decade later.[16]

A new economic agenda

The Reagan administration realized that timing was critical to the success of its economic agenda. With this in mind, President Reagan announced the "Program for Economic Recovery" to Congress immediately after taking his oath of office.[17] The program served to alert both Congress and the public to the new (conservative) administration's primary goals. At the top of the list was a core commitment to reducing marginal tax rates. This was followed by a proposal to reduce the rate of increase in federal spending that would ultimately lead to a balanced budget, expand deregulation, and restrain the money supply to deal with stagflation.[18] Fundamentally, however, Reagan and other Laffer-curve supply-side tax cutters within the cabinet and informal advisors in the Congress embraced the cause of reducing the tax burden on middle-upper-income individuals as the prime component of their agenda for promoting economic growth.

The budget reforms pursued by the Reagan administration beginning in 1981 represented a major shift in the existing tax and spending patterns in the United States.[19] From the onset of Reagan's first term, many economists, members of Congress in both parties, and even members of Reagan's own cabinet began raising red flags regarding the potential dangers that could accompany the president's highly controversial budget. Critics of the president's budget were alarmed about the size of the tax cuts coupled with significant increases in military spending in the midst of a recession. Friction within the cabinet arose out of distinct supply-side camps that existed within the administration itself. According to J. Harold McClure and Thomas D. Willett, "prominent proponents of the radical [Laffer-curve] school included George Gilder, Arthur Laffer, Robert Mundell, Richard Rahn, and Jude Wanniski."[20] Laffer-curve supply-siders, such as these along with others in the US Treasury (e.g., Norman Ture, Craig Roberts, and Steve Entin), proceeded on the basis that supply creates its own demand and that cutting marginal tax rates would create the investment incentives required to boost private economic output substantially. Tax reduction, therefore, became the Laffer-curve supply-siders' single most important priority.[21] Meanwhile, mainstream supply-siders, such as Michael Boskin and Martin Feldstein, asserted "that the basic case for tax and spending cuts and reductions in monetary growth does not depend on the radical [Laffer-curve] supply-side assumption that tax cuts by themselves will raise government revenues and reduce inflation."[22] Although mainstream supply-siders appreciated the importance of tax cuts in providing incentives for growth, such economic leaders as David Stockman, Murray Weidenbaum, and Alan Greenspan saw them operating over the long term and focused instead on reducing government spending as their top priority.[23]

Traditional conservatives, such as Republican Senator Howard H. Baker, in 1981 referred to Reagan's fiscal plan as a "riverboat gamble." Also, David Stockman, Reagan's Office of Management and Budget director at the time, publicly warned the president that his overall budget plan, which called for both highly ambitious tax cuts and massive increases in military expenditure, could have serious consequences for the budget deficit. Initially, however, Stockman was optimistic about the economic recovery and believed that it would produce sufficient revenues to cover the spending increases. As a result, Stockman cautiously endorsed the president's fiscal plan in the 1981 budget meeting. By 1982, however, Reagan's economic program had failed to produce the economic expansion that he had projected, and pressure from those concerned about the budget deficit mounted. As a traditional conservative, Stockman began urging the President to tone down the size of his ambitious tax cuts and advised Reagan to begin aggressive cuts in military expenditure. Adhering to the core principles of his program, Reagan would do neither.

By 1982, the US economy was in a full-blown recession, and the deficit continued to spiral out of control. Faced with these realities, Stockman began to withdraw his support for Reagan's Laffer-curve supply-side strategy. Tired of arguing for spending cuts, Stockman began urging Reagan to raise taxes. Although he personally admitted in his memoirs that his program had been unsuccessful in moving the economy forward in the way he and his core supporters had expected, Reagan nonetheless stood firm in his Laffer-curve supply-side beliefs. Unwilling to yield, Reagan considered not running for reelection rather than to pursue policies that would mean compromising his core policy beliefs.

Reagan's core commitment to reducing taxes and building up the US military led to the ballooning of the deficit by the middle of his second term. The simultaneous pursuit of large tax cuts in conjunction with massive increases in military expenditure during a recession led to budgetary conditions wherein outlays exceeded state revenues. In fact, increases in military spending exceeded the non-defense spending cuts Reagan was able to secure. The change in the profile of federal outlays toward national defense represented a massive shift in policy.[24] Although Reagan received initial support for his early budget proposals from Congress, the recession of 1981 rendered the president's original plan to balance the budget during his first three years virtually impossible to achieve. The downturn in the economy and the resulting decline in tax receipts offset any spending reductions that may have been achieved in non-defense programs. This resulted in the ballooning of the federal deficit to $128 billion in 1982, which in turn set the stage for a string of unprecedented peacetime deficits that would follow.[25]

According to William Niskanen, though the Reagan administration was able to make moderate gains in bringing down real federal spending during its first term in office, spending remained substantially higher than initially projected.[26] The growth of real federal spending during the first term was still substantially higher than the 2.4 percent annual growth of real GNP. "By FY 1985, moreover, real federal spending was 15 percent higher than the initial forecast, about 120 billion in 1985 dollars, and this difference between actual and forecast real spending was almost identical to the increase in the real deficit."[27] The following subsection of this chapter aims to explain the forces that led to this development.

The coalitions, the ideas behind them, and Gramm–Rudman–Hollings

In the early 1980s, at least five significant intrapartisan coalitions were apparent in the US fiscal policy subsystem. They included first the traditional Democratic spenders—proto-Keynesians who strongly believed in the merits of government-driven demand-side strategies for promoting economic growth and full employment. Second were the traditional Republican spenders—a gradually waning group of Nixon-like Republicans who were moderate supporters of proto-Keynesian government-driven policies but were also known to support politically popular tax cuts proposed by the president. Next came Republican tax cutters—Laffer-curve supply-siders led by Ronald Reagan—a radical faction of neoliberals who regarded tax cuts as the best means for restoring private incentives and entrepreneurial initiative. Although viewed as important, fiscal prudence and deficit reduction initiatives were ultimately sacrificed to build the necessary political support for their tax cut plan that was focused on America's wealthiest individual income earners. Republican tax cutters were able to forge a political compromise with Republican spenders in a manner that enabled them to become the dominant faction in the party at the time. Fourth, Republican deficit cutters composed of traditional conservatives and monetarists represented a distinct coalitional faction within the party and believed first and foremost in the need for fiscal prudence and a balanced budget as the core policy issue and in tax reform as an important but secondary issue. They vigorously pursued policy changes that would limit uncontrolled spending. As a relatively smaller voice in the party, they experienced many setbacks in this area in the 1980s. They nevertheless pressed forward with their cause into the 1990s and were ultimately successful in raising the esteem of deficit reduction as a central cause within the Party's political discourse. Last, Democratic deficit cutters composed mainly of monetarists represented a small but cohesive faction of deficit-reduction neoliberals who included a group of conservatives within the party that became known as "blue dog Democrats." Their conservative views made them, in many ways, indistinguishable from their Republican deficit-cutter counterparts (e.g., the partisan crossover of Phil Gramm, TX). Their views on public spending ran counter to the Democratic Party's mainstream Keynesian normative and policy core belief systems. By the 1990s, their neoliberal views on fiscal discipline would come to dominate the party's mainstream agenda under the leadership of Bill Clinton and the new Democrats. Figure 3.1 identifies each of the coalitions and organizes them according to their broad normative core (Keynesian or neoliberal) belief systems and core policy preferences.

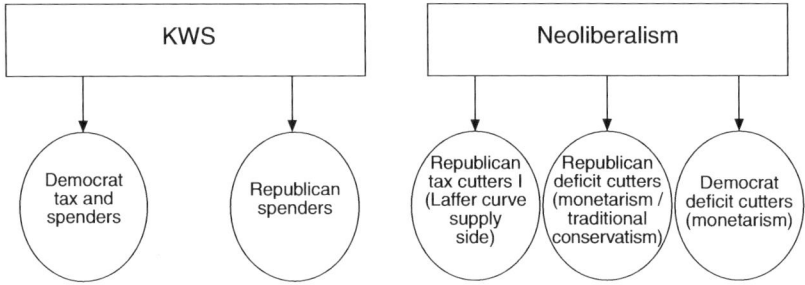

Figure 3.1 Contending subsystem coalitions in the Reagan era

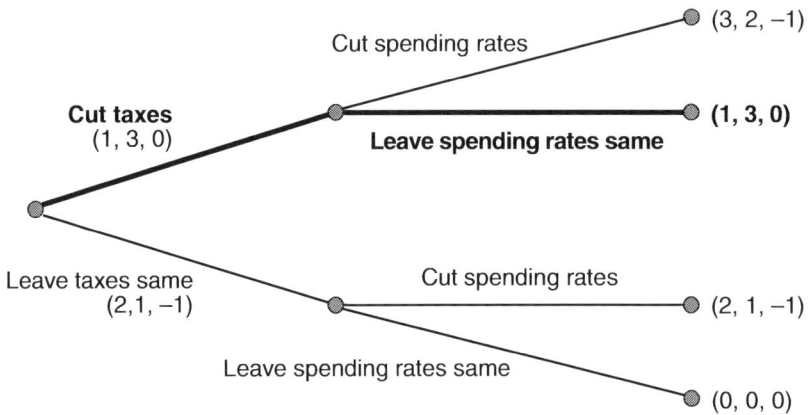

Figure 3.2 Non-cooperative sequential game tree illustrating preference options of significant coalitional players in the fiscal policy subsystem during the Reagan era (1982)

The policy preferences for the five intrapartisan coalitions are presented using a noncooperative three-player sequential game tree in Figure 3.2. As both Republican and Democrat deficit cutters shared critical core policy beliefs regarding the need for fiscal prudence, we have included both under the category of Player 1. Republican tax cutters I are represented as Player 2. Because Democrat and Republican spenders demonstrated little or no support for neoliberal policy change, we have placed them jointly in the category of Player 3. The equilibrium path for the players in this game is indicated by large bold type in the figure. Whenever possible, each coalition in a policy subsystem will pursue strategies that will enable them to realize their respective core as well as secondary policy objectives. That said, deficit cutters in the 1980s sought to pursue cuts in spending as their core objective and tax cuts as their secondary objective. Tax cutters, by way of contrast, would be expected to pursue tax cuts as their core objective and spending cuts as their secondary objective. A coalition is likely to abandon secondary objectives if they come in conflict with core objectives. The conflict that existed between tax cutters and deficit cutters in the 1980s illustrates this point and is reflected in our game tree model. Disagreement over core objectives between tax cutters and deficit cutters led each to pursue divergent neoliberal strategies.

The game tree model illustrates that the highest utility for deficit cutters (Player 1) was to pursue strategies that enabled them to enact tax and spending policies consistent with producing a balanced budget. Where that was not possible, the next best option for deficit cutters was to pursue cuts in spending even at the expense of compromising their (secondary) tax cut objective. If they failed in their main objectives to cut spending rates, deficit cutters could make mild gains if their (secondary) tax cut objectives were realized. Finally, deficit cutters gained nothing if neither core nor secondary objectives were realized.

Given the ambitious size of the tax cuts (meant to be across the board but focused mainly on the rich) sought by Reagan and other tax cutters, reaching a consensus with core deficit cutters was highly unlikely. The best case for tax cutters (Player 2), therefore, was to cut taxes and leave spending patterns unchanged. If tax cutters were to pursue a genuine deficit reduction strategy, they would have no choice but to compromise over the size and structure of their preferred tax cut agenda. If tax cutters failed in their core objective to cut taxes to the degree they desired, the next best strategy for them was to pursue spending cuts, which represented a secondary aspect of their policy agenda. Finally, tax cutters, like deficit cutters gained nothing if tax and spending policies remained unchanged. Therefore, the Nash Solution is that "cut taxes" and "leave spending the same" wins.

What happened to deficit reduction under Reagan

As spending continued to increase throughout the 1980s, Reagan's supply-side agenda came under intense fire by deficit cutters who believed that the administration had reneged on its commitment to achieving a balance budget.[28] Deficit cutters were important partners in the Reagan-led neoliberal consensus and were a group that the administration could no longer afford to ignore. Deficit cutters sponsored an initiative that would compel both Congress and the president to control spending. The Balanced Budget and Emergency Control Act, or Gramm–Rudman–Hollings (GRH), outlined a reduction in spending targets that would eliminate the deficit by 1991.[29] GRH institutionalized the core beliefs of deficit cutters. Although the original deficit reduction targets were ultimately abandoned, supporters of the statute forced lawmakers to consider the urgent need for fiscal discipline in budgetary policy making. GRH opened the policy debate to deficit reduction ideas through a series of public hearings that enabled concerned policy makers and academics alike to express their views and concerns as well as to bring greater public awareness to the issue. These forums were covered by the elite media, whose journalists became a critical conduit in delivering the messages of policy makers, such advocacy groups as Citizens for a Sound Economy, university economists, think tanks, and the like, to the general public regarding the urgent need to deal with the deficit problem. GRH opened both the policy and public discourses to the dangers (i.e. high long-term interest rates and monetary instability) associated with current growth trends in borrowing and spending. Although it proved to have limited legal scope in forcing policy makers to adhere to a balanced budget, the GRH statute helped to bolster the deficit reduction cause to emerge as the single most important budgetary concern in the 1990s.

The GRH initiative, which was formally introduced in 1985, was relatively comprehensive: "[E]verything except [S]ocial [S]ecurity would be subject to across the board cuts or sequestration if the estimated deficit exceeded the target."[30] However, further debate in Congress led to "additional proposals and amendments that ultimately complicated the sequester process."[31] Disagreements between members of Congress and the president persisted over such issues as how much should be cut from domestic programs versus defense and whether taxes should be lowered or increased. A major point of contention for the administration and Congress was the law's provision demanding across-the-board cuts in military and social spending.[32] Deficit reduction was the core issue championed by staunch fiscal conservative deficit cutters, such as Senators Phil Gramm (R-TX) and Warren Rudman (R-NH), whose economic policy concerns were focused on fiscal stability.[33] They believed first and foremost that tax cuts should be matched with cuts in public spending; they were opposed to increasing the deficit.[34]

Most personnel in the first Reagan administration and other Laffer-curve supply-siders in the other offices of government supported the president's tax reduction plan. The source of tension between the two conservative groups was based on differences in their core beliefs. These differences led to a rift in the neoliberal consensus. Hard-core deficit cutters hoped that GRH would compel Reagan and other Laffer-curve supply-siders, along with traditional "tax-and-spend" proto-Keynesians in Congress, to begin serious work to reduce the deficit. Although critical aspects of GRH were not instituted, the "basic thinking" that inspired the initiative continued to endure.[35]

Critics belonging to both the left and right of center raised serious concerns about GRH and its lack of flexibility in allowing increased spending during a recession that might be necessary to initiate an economic recovery.[36] Alas, these differences led to political conditions that made the adoption of GRH in its original form politically unfeasible. In the initial budget that was to be submitted in 1986, Congress passed a resolution that enabled it to attain the GRH deficit target for FY 1987 at $144 billion. President Reagan and his other ardent tax cutter coalition allies rejected the 1986 budget because key provisions contained within it called for a significant tax hike as well as cuts for defense. Democrats in Congress, however, would not allow defense spending to be exempted from the budget cuts, especially when domestic programs were not. This fundamental disagreement resulted in a budget standoff between the White House and Congress that continued into the next fiscal year. Congress responded by adopting a budget as a continuing resolution a month into the fiscal year that was supposed to adhere to the deficit spending limits as established in GRH.

As deficit spending began to exceed initial forecasts, the automatic sequester mechanism established by GRH was enacted. Its life span, however, was short. In 1986, the Supreme Court ruled that the automatic sequestering of federal public spending was unconstitutional. Michael Meeropol brings out that "Congress fixed this by regranting control over the spending cuts or the sequester to the President. The Act remained the law of the land until the Deficit Reduction Act of 1990."[37]

According to Harry Havens, "several years of frustration over the deficit, rising constituent concern, and the absence of any other apparent way to break the stalemate combined to stimulate a ground swell of support for [GRH]."[38] Havens brings out that Senators Dole, Domenici, Packwood (then chairman of the Senate Finance Committee), and Lawton Chiles (ranking Democrat on the Budget Committee) built a consensus to institute the high-profile deficit reduction bill. Havens further reveals that this group "committed themselves to making [the bill] technically workable, predictable in its effects, and perhaps most important, acceptable to the House Democratic leadership."[39] Although the Reagan administration and the Democrat-led Congress were able to reach a consensus on social spending that enabled them to come close to the prescribed spending targets in the late 1980s, the recession of 1990 rendered the original targets virtually unobtainable. In fact, the deficit actually increased and reached more than $250 billion in the early 1990s. William Niskanen argues that although it was modestly lower than that in the previous administration, the growth of real federal spending during Reagan's first term was substantially higher than he initially sought.[40] Niskanen provides a concise summary of federal spending in Reagan's first five years:

> Real federal spending increased at a 3.7 annual rate during the first term, lower than the five percent annual rate during the Carter administration. The growth of real federal spending during the first term was still substantially higher than the 2.4 percent annual growth of real GNP. By FY 1985, moreover, real federal spending was 15 percent higher than the initial forecast, about 120 billion in 1985 dollars, and this difference between actual and forecast real spending was almost identical to the increase in the real deficit.[41]

These numbers caused many to regard the Act and the deficit reduction effort as a whole to be an abject failure. When looked at over the long term however, this does not appear to be the case. When analyzed within a larger context, GRH marked a critical point in the deficit reduction effort.[42] GRH institutionalized the core values of deficit cutters and provided a platform for legitimizing cuts in social spending.

Daniel J. Mitchell brings out that government spending increased as a percentage of GNP between the years 1980 and 1985 by an average of 0.36 percentage points annually.[43] After the adoption of GRH in 1985, however, government spending declined until 1990 by an average of 0.42 percentage points each year since GRH was enacted.[44] The debate surrounding GRH and its passage significantly raised public awareness regarding the dangers of excessive borrowing and the merits of fiscal discipline. GRH raised the visibility of both issues in the fiscal policy discourse.[45] According to Meeropol, "a focus simply on the difference between GRH targets and annual budget deficits ignores important progress in controlling deficits. Since the adoption of GRH the deficit has fallen steadily as a percentage of GNP [and is] far below the path projected prior to the adoption of GRH."[46] James Miller III brings out that one year after the enactment of GRH, "the deficit fell dramatically (from $221 billion in 1986 to $150 billion in 1987)."[47]

The shift in the policy discourse that GRH initiated in the 1980s paved the way for the Budget Enforcement Act of 1990 (BEA). Marvin Kosters brings out that "the BEA was the outcome of several months of contentious 'budget summit' negotiations between senior officials in the Bush administration and congressional leaders during the summer and fall of 1990. The BEA was finally enacted as the Omnibus Budget Reconciliation Act of 1990 (OBRA 1990)."[48] It amended enforcement procedures for budget discipline laid out in both Gramm–Rudman (1985) and the Congressional Budget Act (1974).[49] The OBRA called for tax increases, cuts in projected increases in expenditures under entitlement programs, and a $500 billion reduction in budget deficits over fiscal years 1991 to 1995.[50]

According to James Edwin Kee and Scott V. Nystrom, "the negotiations leading to this agreement considered the status of the deficit and philosophical shift from 'no new taxes' to 'fair taxes'. It led to changes in direct spending, enforcement of budget targets, timing of the budget, sequester usage, tax increases, and entitlement reforms."[51] An important advent of the OBRA was Title XIII, which amended the 1985 version of GRH and became known as the Budget Enforcement Act of 1990. It sought to shift the budget policy focus from annual deficit targets to placing caps on spending by category using three different sequester procedures. The procedures included "mini-sequesters for discretionary items, pay-as-you-go sequesters for direct spending and receipts, and most importantly, the establishment of maximum deficit targets."[52]

Rudolph G. Penner asserts that "viewed as a change in economic policy, the 1990 budget deal was not all that important. But its political significance far exceeded its economic significance. An accurate appraisal of GRH and OBRA requires us to ask what size and shape would modern budgets have taken in their absence."[53] Both GRH and OBRA should be evaluated as to their importance in helping to shape an overall shift in the paradigm discourse toward new fiscal priorities. In Chapter 4, we show how provisions that were established in GRH and OBRA helped to shape deficit reduction in the Clinton era. Specifically, the Clinton administration sought to "test the waters" in Congress for instituting entitlement reforms in cutting cost-of-living adjustments built into Social Security payments. Also, although the automatic sequester functions of the Act were judged to be unconstitutional by the Supreme Court, GRH made deficit reduction and spending restraint the central focus of budget policy in the 1990s.

The reasons behind the Reagan administration's failure to balance the nation's deficit are fairly straightforward, although often inaccurately explained, phenomena. Many accounts simply shed blame on the Democrat-led congress. Although the leaders in the Democratic Party at the time were guided by the logic of Keynes-led spending strategies and by their desire to support popular (and often expensive) social policies in order to get (re)elected, political support for change was lacking from both sides of the aisle. William Niskanen, chair of the Council of Economic Advisers under Reagan, states that in the end "there turned out to be relatively few consistent fiscal conservatives in the administration or in either party in congress."[54] He brings out that many of the smaller programs that comprise the American welfare state were established under the leadership of Republican presidents and were often supported by Republicans in Congress. Niskanen goes on to explain that right-of-center politicians in both parties were more protective of programs that served their own states and favored their own constituencies than they were of those that promoted responsible fiscal policy.[55] Therefore, the enormous growth in the deficit was an unintended result of the Reagan administration's failure to control the growth of overall public spending.[56]

The enormous size of the budget deficit was, in large part, an unintended consequence of Reagan's other tax and spending priorities.[57] Economic conservatives themselves were divided over the deficit issue. Michael Boskin clarifies that *Reaganomics* was a complex mix of neoliberal ideas and policy positions containing preferences that sometimes coincided with one another and sometimes ran counter to one another.[58] In the end "none of the schools got exactly what they wanted." Boskin reveals that such monetarists as Milton Friedman complained bitterly that the Federal Reserve Board's control of the money supply was too erratic, whereas like supply-siders as Paul Craig Roberts complained that the tax cut agenda was not pursued aggressively enough from the very beginning and was ultimately offset by subsequent tax increases.[59] Meanwhile, fiscal conservatives, such as Martin Feldstein, who lauded the administration's efforts to cut domestic spending and reform America's antiquated tax structure, simultaneously expressed grave misgivings about the enormous growth in deficit spending.[60]

Despite Reagan's failure to deliver a balanced budget through Laffer-curve supply-side strategies, all was not lost for deficit cutters. Reagan's broader neoliberal program against big government and big spending was critical to the cause. Through his systematic assaults on the KWS paradigm, Reagan made significant strides in smoothing the path for the introduction of GRH in the policy discourse. Also, although in the 1980s it was less than successful in disciplining government spending to the degree required to balance the budget, GRH represented the first meaningful and serious attempt by politicians in Congress to deal with uncontrolled spending and the ever-increasing budget deficit. GRH forever changed how politicians would approach the subject of deficits and fiscal policy.

Deficit reduction in the Thatcher years

The economic policies pursued by the Thatcher government were instrumental in changing the course of British budgetary politics. The 1980 budget was vital to initiating the economic policy paradigm shift in the government. It introduced a "framework in which public expenditure and taxation were brought together."[61] This framework was part of a broader economic agenda that is known as the *medium-term financial strategy* (MTFS).[62] Despite its neoliberal underpinnings, the landmark provisions contained within the MTFS were quite distinct from the Reagan administration's deficit reduction initiative. The core objective of the MTFS was to bring about economic stability by controlling inflation.[63] The Thatcher–Howe leadership believed, along with their core supporters in the Treasury, that fiscal stability could be obtained only through substantial cuts in the public sector borrowing requirement (PSBR, the national deficit).[64] In contrast to Reagan's rather vague strategies for reducing deficit expenditure, the MTFS contained explicit language about how this would be achieved. It alerted the spending departments and pro-social spending factions within the Tory party, namely the Tory wets, populists, and damps, that tax increases in certain areas would be necessary to pay for existing public programs.[65] The explicit character of the MTFS indicated the strong commitment of Thatcher and her core supporters to solving the deficit problem.

The MTFS represented a major shift from the economic policies pursued by previous governments belonging to both the left and the right of center in Britain's postwar history. Its principal aim was to redirect the policy emphasis from a short-run financial strategy to one that was focused on providing economic stability over an extended period.[66] The main thrust of the strategy centered on reducing the rate of price inflation.[67] To accomplish this, it was believed that a steady reduction in the rate of monetary growth would be required in conjunction with meaningful cuts in both spending and borrowing. Geoffrey Howe sought to institute policies that would lower the rate of monetary growth from the existing seven to eleven percent rate of increase to between four and eight percent by 1983 and 1984. Alec Cairncross brings out that the MTFS was based on the assumption of a "triangular relationship" between broad money (M3), the PSBR (the national deficit), and interest rates. High PSBR rates directly contributed to high nominal interest rates that led to financing difficulties for the private sector.[68] Cairncross states that the MTFS emphasized controlling the growth of the PSBR as a supplement to interest rates in controlling the growth of the money supply. Reducing the size of the PSBR became inextricably linked with monetary policy objectives to keep interest rates at acceptable levels. In so doing, the MTFS "made fiscal policy a corollary of monetary policy when traditionally the management of the economy has rested mainly on fiscal policy with monetary policy as an adjunct to deal with pressure on the balance of payments."[69]

The MTFS was rooted in monetarist principles. Monetary stability was the prime objective of the newly emerging (monetarist) paradigm in Britain. Thatcher and her core supporters in the Treasury embraced monetarist ideas and committed themselves to bringing down interest rates.[70] Thatcher viewed "public expenditure to be at the heart of Britain's economic difficulties."[71] According to Geoffrey Howe, "the four Budgets that were designed in accordance with the MTFS framework (1980–3) succeeded in getting inflation down to four percent by 1983 and in laying the foundation for nine uninterrupted years of economic growth."[72]

The MTFS was more than just a policy strategy. Indeed, it was a comprehensive ideational framework that represented a fundamentally different set of economic beliefs from that of the KWS and the existing tax and spending structure it supported. As is examined more carefully in Chapter 4, the MTFS inspired the Blair government to adopt the *Code for Fiscal Stability*. This was a direct effort to shift fiscal policy goals further from a focus on short-term aims to medium- and long-term consequences.

The foregoing developments mirrored the change that was taking place in academic macroeconomics, which was undergoing a shift from a Keynes-dominated focus on short-term issues toward a long-term focus. Emerging neoliberal studies promoted economic knowledge that emphasized supply side-driven strategies aimed at long-term growth and stability over strategies driven by short-term demand aimed at full employment. The failure of Keynesian policies and academic models to predict and explain persistent hyperinflation, high unemployment, and declining economic growth that occurred throughout the 1970s provided a set of anomalies that eventually led to a full-blown crisis in the existing dominant economic beliefs. These events eventually resulted in a paradigm shift in the academic study of fiscal and monetary policy that was followed in the policy subsystem.

The next major attempt at spending reduction was to come after the 1983 election in the form of Nigel Lawson's first budget as Chancellor of the Exchequer. In contrast to the strategy pursued by the Reagan administration, the first Thatcher–Lawson budget included spending cuts in the area of defense. In the period 1983 to 1984, Lawson was able to secure an agreement with Defence Secretary Michael Heseltine that called for £240 million in defense cuts. Another major breakthrough in defense cuts came again in 1986.[73] These cuts amounted to a significant victory in the name of spending control, as the defense budget represents the largest area of public expenditure by any single governmental department. In the end, Lawson was able to secure cuts in defense spending totaling nearly £500 million.[74] The cuts were made with the intent to institute tax reductions later once the deficit was under control.[75] Despite Thatcher's commitment to pursuing sound monetary goals, she remained steadfast in maintaining institutional control over the Bank of England. Thus, the government would continue to retain formal control over both fiscal and monetary policy. Although the MTFS formally institutionalized the principle of making fiscal policy a corollary of monetary policy, full-blown monetarism with an independent central bank would not be realized in Britain until Tony Blair.

Despite its sound logic, the cuts in public spending initially proposed in the MTFS were not realized. Between 1979 and 1980, the PSBR had already surpassed the initial MTFS target. In fact, government expenditure, which was to have been reduced, actually increased. By the period 1980 to 1981, the PSBR increased to £12.5 billion instead of the £8.5 billion that the government initially outlined.[76] Monetary targets had increased more than 18 percent: "well above the pace of expansion the year before."[77] With respect to institutionalizing core beliefs and policy strategies, Thatcher encountered many of the same difficulties as had Reagan in attempting to cut public expenditure. Policy makers belonging to both the left and right of center in both countries supported the maintenance and growth of the KWS, along with many of its politically desirable domestic programs and social policies.[78]

Differences between the Reagan and Thatcher strategies reflect differences in their core and secondary beliefs. For Reagan, the core issue was tax reduction, whereas for Thatcher it was controlling inflation by pursuing austerity in public expenditure. The logic behind the Thatcher strategy was built on the assumption that cutting public expenditure would lead the way to providing tax cuts that "would somehow release entrepreneurial energies."[79] Despite their varying policy goals and strategies, Thatcher and her supporters in the Treasury, much like the Reagan administration, were forced to settle for less than they initially sought in their quest to cut overall public spending.[80] Alec Cairncross asserts that "when stability even in real terms proved unattainable the Treasury settled for a gradual fall in the ratio of public expenditure to GDP."[81] According to Cairncross, public expenditure (as expressed in real terms) actually increased rapidly after 1979 and had grown by almost 16 percent in the period 1986 to 1987.[82] Cairncross further brings out that despite

> efforts to whittle down benefits by curtailing eligibility and restricting conditions, Thatcher's government was obliged not only to spend heavily on the unemployed but to make increased provision for health, education, and other services. Expenditure on social services and housing (excluding capital expenditure) increased from 36 billion pounds in 1978–9 to 93 billion pounds in 1987–8 or by roughly 30 percent in real terms compared with an increase over the same period in GDP of about 20 percent.[83]

To understand what led to these conditions, we now turn to the discussion of the political environment in which Thatcher and her supporters in the Treasury were forced to contend.

Ideas-based intrapartisan coalitions in the Thatcher era

We can identify at least four significant intrapartisan coalitions within the governing Tory and the opposition Labour Party, all of which were apparent in the fiscal policy subsystem during the Thatcher era. These coalitions included a neoliberal faction of Tory deficit cutters and a Keynesian faction that may be identified as Tory spenders. Also involved in the fiscal policy subsystem arena were two intrapartisan coalitions within the Labour Party: Labour tax and spenders and (to a far less influential degree at the time) the Labour deficit cutters. The two significant Tory coalitions identified here were extracted from Philip Norton's comprehensive analysis of the political, social, and economic factions that comprised the Tory Party in the Thatcher era. Norton identifies eight distinct ideational factions that comprised the Conservative Party in the Thatcher era: *neoliberals, Tory rightists, Thatcher loyalists, party loyalists, populists, wets, drys,* and *damps.*[84] Neoliberal deficit cutters were mainly a group of monetarists made up of neoliberals and Tory rightists. (Thatcher and party loyalists often voted together but were not intellectually committed to her neoliberal cause). Although they are not always clear, the boundaries separating these categories provide a useful way of understanding the distinct ideational forces and groups that were operating within the Tory Party in the Thatcher era. At a time when most of the Tory Party and even Thatcher's own cabinet were considered "wet," Nigel Lawson asserts that "it was the Treasury that Margaret Thatcher ensured was 100 percent dry and on whose support she relied."[85] The term *wet* was used by Margaret Thatcher to refer to those members within the Tory Party who did not share her unswerving commitment to the cause of fiscal discipline.

Margaret Thatcher, who was a true believer in neoliberalism by intellectual persuasion, led a group of sympathizers that included a group that became known as *Thatcherites*; their leading fiscal policy cause was promoting disciplined budgets (in some cases to the point of what critics called *austerity*).[86] Thatcherites were composed of ardent neoliberals like herself as well as others belonging to the Tory right. They believed in the supremacy of the market, supported greater openness in government, and yet were generally opposed to the European Community. Neoliberals included such figures as Christopher Chope, Robert Dunn, Timmothy Eggar, Michael Fallon, Edward Leigh, Michael Portillo, Allan Stewart, Norman Tebbit, John Biffen, William Clark, Geoffrey Howe, Norman Lamont, and Nigel Lawson, among others. Thatcherites belonging to the Tory right emphasized social morality, social order, and discipline and were generally opposed to open government.[87] Individuals identifying with the Tory right, including David Atkinson, Alan

Clark, and David McLean, were attracted to Thatcher's cause to discipline government spending.[88]

While Thatcher loyalists supported Thatcher's bold leadership style, they did not share her strong ideological commitment to neoliberalism.[89] They supported Thatcher because she united the Tory Party by infusing it with a new sense of purpose—to reinvigorate Britain's economy that had long been suffering from industrial decline. Party loyalists, by contrast, were strongly pledged to the Tory Party itself rather than to any particular belief system or any particular party leader.[90] Although she commanded the allegiance of loyalists on both sides on most critical issues, Thatcher was aware that their support was contingent on her ability to lead the party effectively.[91] Loyalist support for Thatcher was most likely assured on politically popular issues and when Thatcher flexed her strength as party leader. She found, however, that when she failed to build broad partisan support in the party, loyalist support for her policies also declined.[92]

Although they identified strongly with the positions of the general population on most issues, populists held less than five percent of the parliamentary vote.[93] They supported capital punishment and immigration control on the one hand, but favored traditional fiscal policies that promoted full employment over monetary stability on the other.[94] As supporters of the KWS, they were wary of Thatcher's privatization scheme. Like Thatcher and her core supporters, populists possessed a strong belief in the need to preserve Britain's economic sovereignty and were, therefore, generally suspicious of the European Community.[95]

Tory wets and damps represented the critics of Thatcherism and the neoliberal course within the Tory Party. Both groups embodied a combination of traditional and progressive members in the party. Although the two groups differed in their level of opposition to the government regarding specific policy issues, they shared beliefs in the need "to maintain stability and harmony of relationships between governors and the governed."[96] Thus, they jointly supported government intervention when necessary and strongly supported the country's involvement in the European Community.[97] They opposed cuts in public spending, the advent of the poll tax, charges for health services, and capital punishment.[98] Figure 3.3 identifies each of the coalitions and organizes them according to their broad normative core (Keynesian or neoliberal) belief systems and core policy preferences.

As with the US case, the policy preference orderings for the three intra-partisan coalitions are shown using a noncooperative three-player sequential game tree in Figure 3.4. Tory deficit cutters (composed of Thatcherite neoliberals and Tory rightists) are represented as Player 1. Tory Spenders (composed mainly of wets, damps, and populists) are represented as Player 2. Finally, Labour tax and spenders are represented as Player 3. As Thatcher loyalists and Tory Party loyalists possessed no specific ideational commitment to any particular fiscal policy strategy, we have not identified those groups in the game model. However, if we were hard pressed to include them, they

```
┌─────────────────────────┐        ┌─────────────────────────┐
│           KWS           │        │      Neoliberalism      │
└─────────────────────────┘        └─────────────────────────┘
```

Labour tax and spenders   Tory spenders   Tory deficit cutters   Labour deficit cutters

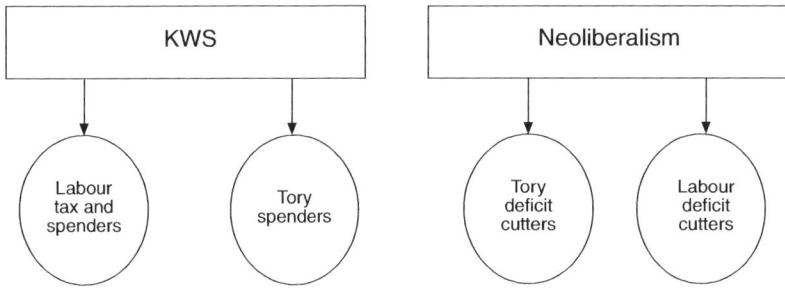

Figure 3.3 Contending subsystem coalitions in the Thatcher era

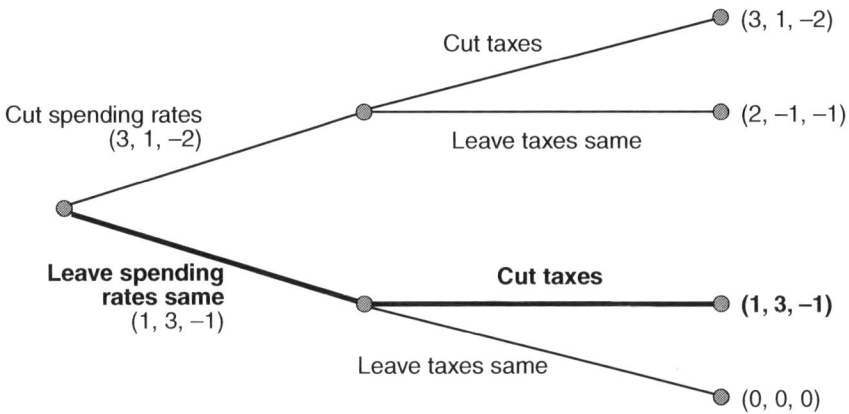

Cut spending rates
(3, 1, –2)

Cut taxes → (3, 1, –2)

Leave taxes same → (2, –1, –1)

Leave spending rates same
(1, 3, –1)

Cut taxes → **(1, 3, –1)**

Leave taxes same → (0, 0, 0)

Figure 3.4 Non-cooperative sequential game tree illustrating preference options of significant coalitional players in the fiscal policy subsystem during the Thatcher era (early 1980s)

would most likely fit under "Player 2" because their level of commitment to the cause of deficit reduction was not very deep. As before, the equilibrium path for the players in this game is indicated by large bold type in the figure. The game tree illustrates that the best scenario for Tory deficit cutters was to pursue strategies that enabled them to enact tax and spending policies consistent with producing a balanced budget. Again, where that was not possible, the next best option for Tory deficit cutters was to pursue cuts in spending even at the expense of compromising their (secondary) tax cut objective. If they failed in their main objective to cut spending rates, deficit cutters could make modest gains if their (secondary) tax cut objectives were realized. Finally, deficit cutters gained nothing if neither their core nor their secondary objectives were realized. Thus the Nash Solution is that "spending remains the same" and "cut taxes" wins. (Please note that any two groups represent majority.)

What happened to deficit reduction under Thatcher

Given the political difficulties associated with gaining support for spending cuts, the deficit cutters again found it difficult to cooperate with Tory spenders. At the same time, Thatcher could not afford to isolate the other factions, such as the wets, populists, and loyalists within the party. The realities of having to spend more rendered it impossible for Thatcher and her core deficit-cutter supporters in the Treasury to build the support necessary for balancing the budget. At the same time, recession-related shortfalls in the Treasury meant that deficit cutters would have no choice but to scale down the size of their tax cut agenda, a secondary issue, if they were to make a serious attempt at reducing the PSBR. As a result, deficit cutters, led by Thatcher and her core supporters in the Treasury, had to settle for modest gains in both their tax and spending preferences.

The Thatcher government was heavily constrained from the very beginning in its ability to cut public spending by preexisting structures, institutions, beliefs, political pressures, and Party manifesto commitments. According to Nigel Lawson, long-term pressures for higher public spending came "from the aging of the population, the development of costly technologies, the lobbying of vested interests the innate desirability of many of the forms of public expenditure, the inherent desire of all bureaucracies to expand their empires, and the failure to recognize that what is provided free still has to be paid for."[99] Despite these constraints, however, Lawson was convinced that it was still ultimately possible to reduce public expenditure as a share of GDP. Lawson asserts that "where previous Conservative governments (with the rather special exception of a few years in the early 1950s, when defense spending was greatly reduced following the end of the Korean War) had merely succeeded in slowing down the seemingly inexorable onward march of the State, the Thatcher Government, by single-minded determination, succeeded in reversing it."[100]

According to Lawson, although cuts in the growth of public spending began under the Wilson–Callaghan governments of the 1970s (mainly under pressure from the International Monetary Fund (IMF)), they had no significant affect on the public spending ratio, given simultaneous declines in the level of economic growth that occurred in the same time frame.[101] Lawson clarifies that although public spending increased slightly under the first three parliaments led by Thatcher, economic growth increased substantially, leading to a reduction in the spending ratio by two full percentage points.[102] According to Lawson, the Thatcher government succeeded in slowing down "the seemingly inexorable onward march of the state" by adhering to a clear set of spending priorities in the face of fierce conflict among rival interests.[103] Critical cuts were achieved in such areas as transport, trade and industry, and housing subsidies and support.[104] By way of contrast, such areas as law and order, employment and training, and health, which were clear policy priorities for the Thatcher government, had their funding increased.[105] In addition, the number of individuals drawing on public benefits had been steadily increasing over the previous decade.[106] This was largely the result of unemployment caused by deindustrialization, a phenomenon over which Thatcher and her core supporters in the Treasury obviously had little control. Steady growth in the pensioner population, dramatic increases in the number of single-parent families, and increasing numbers of families that became reliant on means-tested welfare benefits caused by growing industrial unemployment meant that social security welfare spending had to be substantially increased as well.[107]

Although her government ultimately accepted spending increases over the decade as a whole, Thatcher managed crucial cuts in public policy areas, such as employment training, where private sector alternatives were more available.[108] According to Lawson, these cuts represented a watershed in the process toward spending retrenchment that would serve as the basis for later cuts at the end of the period when private profitability recovered and public–private cooperatives were developed involving sizable private-sector funding.[109] Competition among rival spending interests intensified as Thatcher pushed for cuts in public expenditure in an effort to eliminate the PSBR. In so doing, Thatcher and her core supporters in the Treasury courted a war with the spending ministers, made up of Tory spenders, who began making strong appeals against these spending cuts in the PESC-Star Chamber, in an effort to protect their turf.[110] Geoffrey Howe called for a comprehensive review in which the cabinet authorized the Central Policy Review Staff (CPRS), led by Alan Bailey, to investigate options for reducing spending.[111] Howe presented a paper based on the CPRS's survey predicting that public expenditure would remain at 47 percent of GDP for the next 10 years.[112] This was three percent higher than that in Labour's last year in power.[113] Howe responded by pressing for a fundamental reexamination of public expenditure and proposed what many regarded at the time as extreme "rightist" remedies.[114] Such "remedies" included "education vouchers in place of 'free' state schools, increases in the pupil–teacher ratio, the replacement of part of the National Health Service (NHS) by compulsory private health insurance, and the cancellation of the Trident missile program."[115] Lawson brings out that though Howe insisted that the proposals were based on sound and sober analyses conducted by the Treasury, the result was the nearest thing to a cabinet riot in the history of the Thatcher government. According to Lawson, "this episode played into the hands of the 'wets'."[116] The wets not only managed to get the CPRS report shelved at the meeting but made sure that its contents were leaked to *The Economist*, which obligingly described it as "dismantling huge chunks of the welfare state."[117] The leadership in the Labour Party responded incisively by alleging in the 1983 election that the Tory's had adopted a "secret manifesto" and, in the final days of the campaign, the Labour shadow Chancellor, Peter Shore, released a full text of the CPRS report in an effort to build political support against Thatcher's retrenchment agenda.[118]

The Thatcher government courted additional political resistance in 1984 when Sir Keith Joseph and Chief Secretary Peter Rees sought to increase substantially funding for university science research budgets by abolishing the minimum maintenance grant paid to all parents regardless of means. The new policy would require wealthier parents to pay a means-tested contribution toward the tuition as one remedy to reduce pressure on public spending.[119] This proposal met with considerable political opposition. According to Lawson, "the real problem was the people who would be hurt by the proposed changes were not the poor, who were fully protected, nor the rich, who could take the increased parental contributions in their stride, but the people in between.[120] They were the people who constituted the bulk of the Party activists in the constituencies and, in particular, the local Party officers."[121] As result of these episodes, Thatcher had no choice but to respond by scaling down her attacks on the welfare state.

Tax reform in the Reagan–Thatcher era

Differences in core and secondary aspects of Reagan and Thatcher's policy beliefs explain their divergent neoliberal experiments with tax reform. Reagan's apparent undiscerning pursuit of tax cuts and increased military expenditure caused him to treat the cause of deficit reduction with benign neglect in the 1980s. Thatcher, by way of contrast, deliberately increased the value added tax from the very beginning in an effort to cover any revenue loss that resulted from her government's personal income tax cuts. Despite these differences, both the Reagan and Thatcher administrations introduced a series of major reforms that led to the restructuring of the tax systems in the United States and Britain.

As stagflation and slow growth ensued throughout the 1970s in the United States and Britain, neoliberals asserted that the redistributive tax system was in need of fundamental reform. Michael Boskin asserts that "by the early 1980s, a growing number of policymakers were convinced that the US tax system had reached a crisis and was in dire need of fundamental reform."[122] Experts pointed to substantial declines in net investment and production facilities as inflationary pressures, rather than real increases in income, pushed both businesses and individuals into higher marginal tax brackets.[123] Boskin reveals that "the fraction of the population subject to very high marginal tax rates had quadrupled between 1965–80 ... and the top marginal tax rate on investment was much higher (70 percent) than it was on earnings (50 percent)."[124] Tax cutters grew increasingly concerned that the existing tax system discouraged savings and investment—the very ingredients that economic experts asserted were necessary for economic growth.[125]

In Britain, Thatcher and her advisers believed that poor economic performance stemmed, in large part, from Britain's "inefficient and nominally progressive tax system."[126] The Conservative leader blamed high tax rates for declining levels of domestic investment. Here again, however, tax reform was meant to be only one component (albeit an important one) of a broader economic strategy that was focused primarily on promoting monetary and fiscal stability. According to Sven Steinmo, this represented a sharp contrast with the Reagan administration's policies whereby "the conflict between these two objectives was ignored."[127]

Tax reform in the Reagan era

The central goal of Reagan and the Laffer-curve supply-siders' initial economic program was to reduce the tax burden in the United States. According to Steinmo, "the main features of the initial proposal were approved by Congress in 1981 and survived subsequent changes in federal tax law in each of the next three years."[128] When examined in tandem, the tax reforms enacted throughout the Reagan era represent a fundamental shift in the course of US tax policy.[129] It is important to understand, however, that these reforms were not always coherent. In fact, at times, they even produced results that were incompatible with the broader goals of the neoliberal agenda. The increase in the budget deficit was a byproduct of Reagan's initial tax reforms and increases in military spending.[130] According to Niskanen, Reagan's benign neglect of the deficit issue stemmed from the fact that although it had a clear tax agenda, his administration did not have a coherent deficit-reduction strategy.[131]

ERTA, TEFRA, the 1986 Tax Reform Act, and all that

As the first major piece of domestic legislation signed by President Reagan, the Economic Recovery Tax Act (ERTA) of 1981 set the stage for a sequence of reforms that would follow.[132] According to Niskanen, "ERTA became the centerpiece of Reaganomics both for its supporters and its critics."[133] In proposing a 30 percent cut in personal income taxes, the coalition of tax cutters that supported the Act had severely challenged reigning beliefs governing the existing tax and spending system. It also established an automatic indexation of tax brackets that would adjust to the cost of living. In a larger sense, enacting the ERTA served to provide a certain validation for the administration's broader neoliberal goals of reducing government interference in the private sphere.

Despite praise from tax cutters, Reagan's policies came under increasing attack from the deficit cutters owing to revenue loss and associated increases in the budget deficit. The Treasury Department's Office of Tax Analysis estimated a revenue loss totaling $323 billion or 5.6 percent of GDP from 1983 to the beginning of the next decade.[134] In an effort to address growing concerns about the budget deficit, the Reagan administration called for significant tax increases for FYs 1982 and 1983.[135] Niskanen brings out that Office of Management and Budget director David Stockman and other key presidential staff began working with Republican leaders in the US Senate, such as Pete Domenici (R-NM) and Robert Dole (R-KS), to reach a prudent budget agreement known as the Tax Equity and Fiscal Responsibility Act (TEFRA). In the final analysis, the Reagan administration supported a tax increase of $95 billion as long as "it did not revise the individual income tax cuts approved in 1981."[136] According to Michael Boskin, "TEFRA 'took back' about 25 percent of the tax cuts instituted by ERTA. Nevertheless, the net impact by fiscal year 1988 was still to be a $215 billion tax reduction."[137]

Reagan came to understand that pursuing across-the-board tax cuts while significantly expanding the military budget in the midst of a recession would make balancing the budget a very difficult proposition to uphold. Having achieved marked gains in core aspects of his tax cut agenda, Reagan turned to an important issue that represented a secondary aspect of his policy beliefs: deficit reduction. This is important because Laffer-curve supporters held that there should have been no conflict between reducing taxes and cutting the deficit. When this proved not to be the case, the administration made revisions in secondary aspects of its policy beliefs.

Although deficit cutters expressed serious concerns over revenue loss caused by the ERTA, an increasing number of critics also questioned the ERTA's effectiveness in protecting and encouraging investment. According to Niskanen, "[T]here were still considerable differences in the effective tax rates on income from different types of investment, differences that may not reflect the objectives of public policy, and these differences increased with the rate of inflation."[138] The restructured tax code failed to remove incentives for debt financing, and tax rates on business investment loomed higher than those on individual earnings. Disenchanted stakeholders—composed of business investors, monetarists, conservatives, and tax cutters in the Congress —jointly pushed for deeper reforms that would seriously address these shortcomings.

The Tax Reform Act of 1986

The Tax Reform Act of 1986 was enacted in an effort to deal with concerns raised by the ERTA's critics. In the quest to recover losses that occurred under the ERTA, deficit cutters pressed for further reforms that would directly address the deficit issue. According to Meeropol, the Tax Reform Act of 1986 differed from the ERTA in the sense that it was not a tax cut.[139] In an effort to address deficit reduction concerns seriously, Reagan insisted that tax cuts now be "revenue-neutral." That is to say, cuts in one area of the tax code had to be offset by increases in another. Further, Meeropol asserts that "lower published rates were paid for by abolishing a number of preferences including those that could be used to shelter income ... [which] had the effect of raising the marginal tax rate on a number of high income individuals and actually increasing the effective rate on many businesses."[140]

The 1986 Tax Reform Act was enacted to reduce tax rates while widening the tax base.[141] With these goals in mind, the Treasury proposed what Michael Boskin asserts is "the most sweeping individual and corporate income tax reforms in US history."[142] The Act reduced the number of tax brackets from the existing 14 to 4 while reducing the average individual income rate by 6.1 percent.[143] It shifted the tax burden from personal to corporate income tax, which would create $100 billion in revenue over five years. According to Michael Boskin, the new burden would be shared among shareholders, workers, and consumers.[144] It further resulted in the elimination of the investment tax credit, a reduced corporate rate of 34 percent, and a maximum personal rate of 28 percent.[145]

According to William Niskanen, the overall effect of these reforms fundamentally changed marginal tax rates for all income groups.[146] Niskanen concludes that, when compared with marginal tax rates from the beginning of the decade with those from 1984, tax rates were lowered by approximately five percent in the case of low-income families, increased by almost six percent for median-income families, and reduced by about 12 percent for higher-income families.[147]

Tax reform in the Thatcher era

As brought out earlier, the MTFS provided the basic framework for tax and spending policies over an extended period of time.[148] The budget of 1980–1 represented a fundamental shift in the structure of tax policy in Britain. As one of its first policy initiatives, the Thatcher government consolidated the existing national sales value added tax (VAT) system, which had originally contained two rates (12.5 percent for luxury items and a lower rate of eight percent on everything else), into a single rate of 15 percent.[149] Thatcher realized that she had to enact the VAT reform in the first budget if she was to ensure its success.[150] The prime minister understood the symbolic importance of enacting a major piece of tax reform early on so as to set strong precedent for instituting a host of other neoliberal policy changes, namely reduction of the PSBR.[151]

Thatcher and loyalist supporters both inside and outside the Treasury believed that a major reduction in income tax was needed to restore incentives.[152] However, Thatcher's core commitment to reducing the nation's deficit meant that the government had to find other sources of revenue to comply with existing budgetary constraints. According to Nigel Lawson, the decision to increase the VAT to 15 percent in 1979 was "a contentious decision" that invited resistance not only from the Labour Party but from wets, damps, and populists within the Tory Party itself.[153] Even sympathizers in the London Business School and some monetarists, such as Samuel Brittan, argued "that the increased rate would fuel inflationary expectations, give a fill-up to a gathering wage explosion and increase the unemployment cost of reducing inflation."[154]

Thatcher was able to cultivate support within various groups (populists, wets, and drys) of the Tory Party to enact a series of important reforms that fundamentally altered the tax structure in Britain. One of the most widely expressed goals of the Tory Party was to reduce the tax burden on Britain's upper-income individuals.[155] Thatcher led an incisive attack on the redistributive logic intrinsic in the existing tax system. According to Sven Steinmo, the Tories sought immediate relief for England's better off "whose increased superfluity would in their view, have the greatest effect on the overall health of the economy."[156] Reducing the tax burden on wealthy individuals represented an area in which Thatcher's and Reagan's policies were highly consistent with one another. Both realized that high state income tax rates meant that high-income earners would spend the most resources on sheltering income. All these expenditures were viewed to be purely rent-seeking in nature and were thus regarded as a total waste for the whole economy. Both leaders reasoned that their countries' tax systems needed to be restructured in a manner that decreased the burden on personal income.[157] Over a period of 12 years, Thatcher delivered substantial cuts in the marginal income tax rate, reducing the top rates on the highest income brackets from 98 to 40 percent and reduced the bottom rates from 33 to 25 percent.[158]

Over the 1979–91 period, the Thatcher government introduced significant cuts in capital gains taxes and abolished both the investment income surcharge and social security (National Insurance) surcharges imposed on employers altogether.[159] The Thatcher government also initiated dramatic cuts in income taxes while increasing taxes on personal allowances in 1987 and 1988. Steinmo reveals, however, that by the turn of the decade, recession-related fiscal constraints forced the Conservative government to tone down its ambitious tax-cutting agenda.[160]

The Thatcher–Lawson government launched a major effort devoted to reforming the existing corporate profit tax structure. In spite of the fact that the Thatcher government increased VAT, instituted the highly controversial poll tax, and levied new taxes on North Sea oil profits to pay for tax cuts to employers and investors, the government, particularly in the Lawson years, also sought major reforms in corporate taxation. Encouraging financial investment was the paramount goal of the Thatcher government, and its tax policies were designed in accordance with that end. Interestingly, both Thatcher and Reagan ended up pursuing reforms that actually led to increases in the overall corporate tax burden in their respective countries.

As savings and investment declined throughout the decade, policymakers increasingly came to believe that tax policies governing corporate profits, which had been designed in the Keynesian era, were the major culprit in causing investment flight and economic decline. According to Steinmo, "[T]he problem with corporate taxes in Britain, from the government's point of view, was not that companies paid too much in taxes, but rather that the incentive structure provided by the preexisting tax system encouraged investment in manufacturing sectors over financial and portfolio institutions."[161] The Conservative government, therefore, sought systematically to reconstruct Britain's tax policy in such a way that would remedy this. Steinmo brings out that

[T]he reform contained many components: corporate taxes were reduced from 52 percent to 35 percent for large companies and from 42 percent to 25 percent for smaller companies; major investment incentives and stock relief deductions were removed or reduced; corporate capital gains were indexed; the National Insurance surcharge was abolished; stamp duties on stock and bond transfers were halved; and finally the investment income surcharge was eliminated.[162]

When taken as a whole, these reforms were a fundamental shift in Britain's taxation system. They established an entirely new foundation for investment and corporate decisions by radically altering the tax distortions that were believed to have been responsible for disinvestment and economic decline. Despite the Thatcher government's sincere efforts to produce the opposite effect, the corporate tax reforms ultimately led to overall increased tax levies on British companies. This unintended outcome stemmed from the fact that the reforms lacked coherence because they were designed in the absence of any sustained analysis. Steinmo brings out that the reforms were rash solutions to immediate problems that were created in virtual secrecy by a handful of top-level ministers in the Treasury.

Although both Reagan's and Thatcher's tax reform initiatives were directed at restructuring the existing tax structure, important differences existed between the policy strategies each pursued. These differences reflect differences in the relative priority that each administration placed on tax reform versus fiscal-monetary stability. Although both Thatcher and Reagan pursued different tax strategies, their governments ended up increasing the overall corporate tax burden in their respective countries. If policy success is measured by an administration's ability to institutionalize the core and secondary aspects of its belief system, tax reforms introduced by Reagan and Thatcher can be regarded as a mixed victory. Although both leaders were able to introduce major reforms in their countries' tax structure, the most important consequence of the Reagan–Thatcher tax reform effort is that it represented an acute assault on one of the most important redistributive engines of the KWS. The overall effect of their policies served to redistribute the tax burden in a regressive direction. The underpinning logic behind Reagan's economic agenda was the notion that reducing the marginal tax rates would spur entrepreneurial activity and economic growth.[163]

Although playing an important role in Thatcher's neoliberal agenda, tax reform remained a secondary aspect of it. Thatcher and her core supporters in the Treasury believed that economic growth depended fundamentally on controlling the growth of the money supply and public spending.[164] Following a monetarist prescription of fiscal austerity, Thatcher insisted that tax cuts in one area be funded through increases imposed somewhere else. This was demonstrated by the fact that while Thatcher sought to cut taxes on upper-income individuals, she raised VAT and instituted the infamous poll tax in expectation that these advents would offset any loss of revenue that might augment the deficit.

Conclusion: the United States and Britain compared

The tax reform efforts in the United States and Britain were organized around a distinct set of principles. Reagan and other Laffer-curve supply-side tax cutters in the cabinet and Congress led the tax reform effort in the United States. At the same time, they were supported by a variety of subsystem actors, including business groups and certain think tanks. Although Reagan was against monetary expansion, the tax reform strategy ultimately accepted by his administration proved to be rather narrow—one aimed principally at reducing personal income taxes. By way of contrast, the tax reform effort pursued under Thatcher was meant to be designed in accordance with a broader monetarist fiscal strategy.

Unlike many of the political stigmas that were associated with spending cuts and deficit reduction, tax reform was a very appealing proposition supported by members belonging to the left and right of center in both the United States and Britain. In the United States for example, the Democrat-led Congress actually approved tax cuts that went beyond what the Republican administration initially proposed.[165] In Britain, the idea of tax reform enjoyed wide support by groups all over the political landscape, particularly from the City to middle-class England.

Cultivating a consensus for reform is always a difficult process and hardly ever results in total agreement on all points of prior discord. Thus, the case of tax reform during the Reagan–Thatcher era is no exception. Deficit cutters expressed serious misgivings over increased government spending and its effects on long-term interest rates.[166] At the same time, Reagan and other Laffer-curve supply-siders in the United States "made a revenue-generating tax reform politically out of the question ..."[167] The Reagan administration introduced a series of reforms whereby "marginal income-tax rates were reduced rapidly, depreciation was accelerated, and savings incentives were made universal."[168]

Although supply-siders were the front-runners in the pursuit of tax reform in the United States, monetarists and conservatives were not far behind. In fact, these groups lauded the proposition of reducing the overall tax burden in the United States. Rather, their concerns mirrored those of the Thatcher administration: how the proposed tax reform would affect the deficit. Given the electoral rewards that would likely accompany tax breaks to the American public, it is not surprising that members of Congress belonging to both the left and right of center ended up supporting the resulting tax reform agenda. Rather, it is resulting rises in corporate tax policy that requires explanation.

Despite the fact that Reagan and Thatcher exhibited varying levels of commitment to the issue of corporate tax reform, in the end the policies pursued by both governments actually led to overall increases in the corporate tax burden in both countries. This is particularly evident in the case of the United States, where cuts in individual income taxes were ultimately funded by imposing greater tax burdens on corporate income. Executive leaders and their coalition partners will attempt to use a variety of means ranging from bargaining to coercion to institutionalize both core and secondary aspects of their belief systems. On occasion, however, executive leaders may be compelled to compromise over secondary aspects of their belief systems to guarantee the success of core aspects of their agenda. In signing the final tax bill that caused the shifting of the tax burden to corporate profits, Reagan compromised the secondary aspects of his neoliberal fiscal policy agenda to preserve a core aspect: reducing the tax burden on personal income.

Although it differed from the Reagan administration in its corporate tax reform strategies, Thatcher's government also enacted policies that actually increased the burden on corporate income. In pluralist democracies, wherein a variety of subsystem actors are involved in the implementation of any major tax change (e.g., various Treasury departments, the Inland Revenue, relevant parliamentary committees, and the like) and many more (e.g., business community, private investors) are directly affected by them, the importance of deliberative consultation is often necessary for ensuring policy success. As brought out earlier, Sven Steinmo correctly asserts that the 1984 reforms were designed in virtual secrecy without the benefit of sustained analysis and any deliberative input from critical actors in the broader subsystem arena. Simply stated, the reforms of 1984 present a textbook case of how the absence of reasoned discourse and consultation led to unintended outcomes.

Reagan and Thatcher found that members in their own governments were deeply divided over the deficit issue. As a result, both were unable to cultivate a consensus to bring about the substantial reductions in government spending that would have been required to meet their initial deficit reduction targets. In spite of this, Reagan's and Thatcher's pioneering efforts laid the foundation that initiated the shift in the public's understanding of the deficit issue. Nigel Lawson confirms that "in terms of fundamental aims the MTFS succeeded [and] that there can be no doubt that the MTFS came to play a central role in the Government's economic policy."[169] Reagan and Thatcher set in motion the neoliberal wheels that provided the political momentum for the deficit reform efforts that would continue under their left-of-center rivals by Clinton and Blair almost a decade later.

4 Deficit reduction and tax reform under Clinton and Blair

Neoliberal ideas and the Clinton–Blair connection

This chapter compares the fiscal policy beliefs and policies of Clinton and Blair. An intensive study of these leaders and the neoliberal ideas that guided them has led us to four important conclusions. First, highly similar fiscal strategies pursued by the Clinton and Blair administrations reflect strong continuities in their core and secondary policy beliefs. Second, the policy strategies followed by Clinton, Blair, and Thatcher were inspired (to varying degrees) by monetarism, whereas those followed by Reagan were based on Laffer's supply-side approach. Third, Clinton's and Blair's success in getting the spending cuts necessary to balance the budget in the United States and Britain stems, in large part, from the fact that they were able to build broad political support within the fiscal policy subsystem. Fourth, for Clinton and Blair, fiscal prudence represented a core aspect of their of policy beliefs as evidenced by the fact that both leaders spent tremendous amounts of political capital toward that effort. Neoliberal tax policy initiatives—a secondary aspect of their policy beliefs—pursued by Clinton and Blair would be designed in accordance with their highest economic priority: deficit reduction.

When Clinton came to power in 1993, the deficit was the most pressing item on the political agenda, and it represented a core issue for the new administration.[1] The urgency to solve the deficit problem stemmed from its recession-related surge at the end of the Bush administration. President George H. Bush's contentious decision to raise taxes on upper-income individuals in 1990 demonstrates the importance of the deficit reduction issue in the political discourse at that time. Bush's tax hike symbolized a break with Reagan's Laffer-curve supply-side approach. By the 1992 election, neoliberal claims that spending proclivity was responsible for economic decline were resonating strongly with voters.[2] It was clear that governments, regardless of their ideological persuasion, would have to commit themselves to the cause of fiscal stability above all other budgetary goals. The ballooning of the deficit to nearly \$300 billion under Reagan–Bush made it clear that subsequent administrations that sought to eliminate deficit expenditure would have to spend enormous amounts of political capital toward that effort. This would mean putting deficit reduction ahead of any other fiscal goal.

Within six years of taking office, the Clinton administration was able to deliver what 12 years of uninterrupted Republican control of the White House under Reagan and Bush could not: a balanced budget. Most important, however, was the new fiscal course that the administration set in motion. Even by the most conservative estimates, the spending trends that the Clinton administration established were expected to create a cumulative fiscal surplus totaling more than half a trillion dollars over 10 years.[3] This would be an unprecedented achievement in US fiscal policy. The US economic expansion of the 1990s was by far the longest in its history. Lasting more than 10 years, it was twice as long as the average expansionary cycle of the post-World War II era. This, of course, generated very high tax revenues that helped to reduce the reliance on deficit spending as a source of funding.

One must look at the contributing causes of the expansion itself. To be sure, dynamic growth in the high-tech service sector and the enormous increases in the value of the NASDAQ along with the growth of other sectors that followed on its coattails were all major factors. Additionally, anemic economic conditions in Europe and financial crises in East Asia, Russia, and Latin America led to massive capital flight caused by nervous investors in search of more stable and secure markets. The result was an unexpected flood of new foreign investment in US capital markets that helped to produce the boom in new service technology industries. Strong executive leadership and guidance in the budget process were essential in setting a fiscal agenda that was consistent with producing a low-inflation economic environment. These conditions provided strong incentives to foreign investors to redirect their money away from countries whose lax fiscal and monetary policies were believed to have led to economic turbulence and in favor of the United States.

The fact that this massive economic expansion occurred in the absence of any "government-managed stimulus program" proved to be the final death blow to the Keynesian welfare state (KWS) and its basic causal assumptions regarding the need for state spending to resolve macroeconomic dilemmas. This had the consequence of bolstering political support for the deficit reduction cause in the fiscal policy subsystem. The sheer magnitude of the recovery itself provided the ultimate vindication of the neoliberal paradigm in the United States.

Clinton's neoliberal roots can be traced all the way back to the welfare reform effort of 1987 when he chaired the National Governors' Association. Clinton played a highly active role in federally instituting *workfare*, which became a central component of President Reagan's *Family Support Act*. The then-governor asserted that "every welfare recipient should sign a contract with the state, making a personal commitment in return for benefits to pursue an individually developed path to independence."[4] Clinton sought to build on these neoliberal themes in his bid for the presidency in 1992.

The election of Bill Clinton in 1992 signified the rise to power of "new Democrats." Clinton and other centrists in the Democratic Leadership Council (DLC), such as Al Gore, Al From, Dave McCurdy, Will Marshall, Ed Kilgore, Joseph Lieberman, and others, sought to redefine the party's basic policy ideas in line with neoliberal thinking. Clinton and the DLC's normative core beliefs revered market principles and preferred them to government-led redistribution. Clinton and the DLC abandoned the traditional Democratic paradigm and preached the virtues of individual responsibility and accountability in place of "collective welfare." *Clintonites* advocated substituting a policy of workfare, the marriage between labor skill development and public assistance for the unemployed, in place of traditional welfare dependency.[5]

Neoliberal principles had been steadily capturing the support of America's middle-class voters going back to the time of Reagan. The DLC's belief in fiscal and individual responsibility, for example, was an integral part of "middle-class" values in the 1990s. By the time the New Democrats took control of the White House in 1993, welfare retrenchment and smaller government, especially with respect to deficit reduction, had become the defining issues for America's middle class.

Middle-class support was critical to the success of the new Democrats in 1992. Recapturing middle-class voters who had fled to the Republican Party in the 1980s (the so-called Reagan Democrats) meant changing the party's affiliation with class-based policies and political rhetoric toward more middle-class views, policies, and electoral strategies. The core support of Roosevelt's New Deal compromise, the basic logic of which sustained the party up until the 1970s (and in some sense as late the 1980s), was the political group that was identified as America's "working class." However, over time, fewer and fewer Americans had been identifying themselves with the working class and the traditional Democratic political agenda affiliated with it. In the 1950s, two-thirds of those who described themselves as working class were supporters of the Democratic Party. Today, however, less than 50 percent of the population describes itself as working class. Additionally, even though the Democratic Party has for the last 50 years consistently received between 60 and 70 percent of the working-class vote, the weight of the working class has inevitably declined. Members of the middle and upper classes comprise 45 percent of those who identify themselves as members of the Democratic Party. Figure 4.1 shows the trend line in working-class and middle-class Democratic Party identification.

This shift accompanies the phenomenon of economic transformation from an industry-based economy to a service-based one. Economic transformation has reduced the value of union support to the Democratic Party, as the proportion of party identifiers with a union membership in their family has fallen from 27 to 17 percent over the last 40 years. Also, although union families remain loyal to the Democratic Party, the proportion of Democratic Party identifiers has fallen from one-third to one-fifth. As

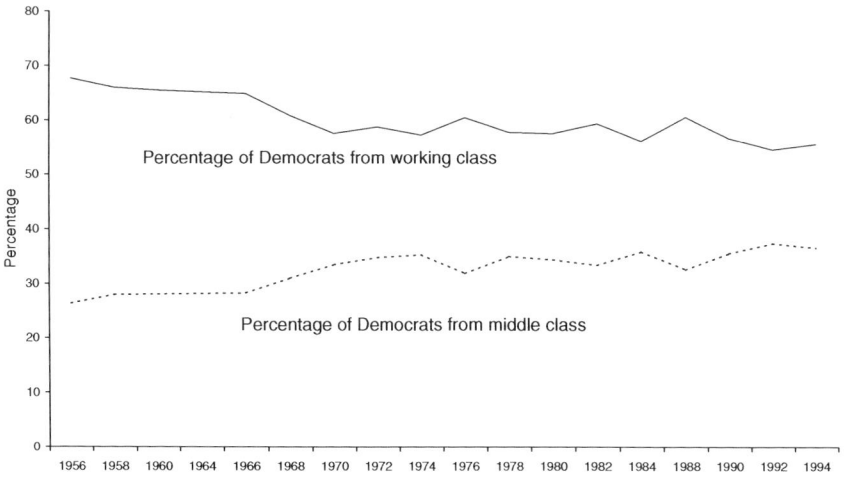

Figure 4.1 Social class and Democratic Party identification, 1956–94
Source: American National Election Studies, 1956–94

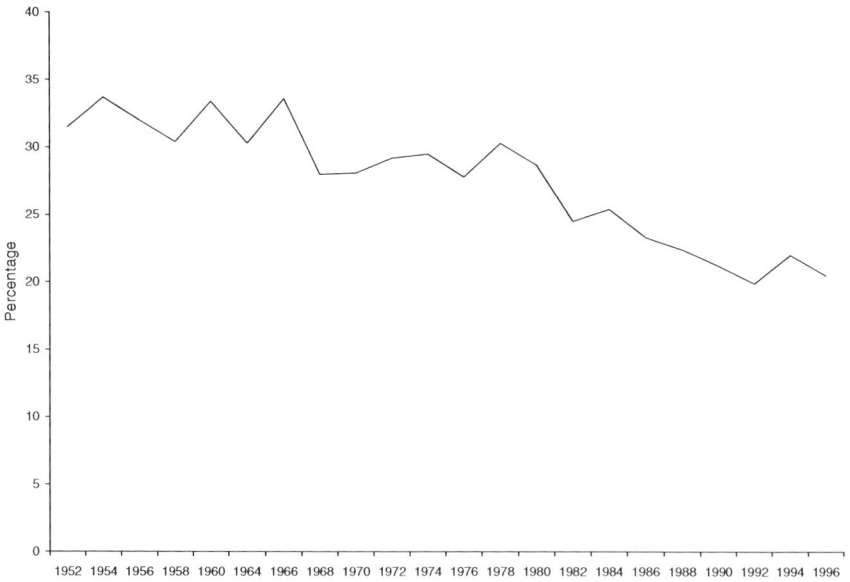

Figure 4.2 Percentage of Democratic Party identifiers from a Union family, 1952–96
Source: American National Election Studies, 1952–96

shown in Figure 4.2, the period of the sharpest decline was in the 1980s, when both the consequences of economic transformation and a hostile political environment for unions led to a rapid reduction in the rate of union membership.

Much the same way, 20 years ago over 30 percent of the jobs in Britain were in manufacturing and less than 60 percent were in service industries. Today less than 20 percent of the jobs are in manufacturing and more than 70 percent are in service industries. Faced with a very similar experience of economic transformation and consequent shifts in electoral attitudes that had been taking place as early as the 1970s in Britain, modernizers in the British Labour Party had long sought to adopt a new set of economic ideas and strategies that could be successfully translated into a middle-class-oriented political agenda of their own. The miraculous economic expansion of the United States in the 1990s directly influenced the thinking of policy makers across the Atlantic. Impressed by the success of new Democrats to move their party to the political center, modernizers early on established a close relationship with Clinton and his cabinet. Although neoliberal ideas had been gaining support in the Labour Party since the *Policy Review* was established in the 1980s, the Blair government's commitment to a balanced budget was heavily reinforced by the US experience under Clinton's leadership. Similarities in the fiscal policy strategies pursued by the Clinton and Blair administrations stemmed from their commitment to a shared set of core and secondary policy beliefs. Most important, Clinton's and Blair's success in eliminating deficit spending and the dynamics that led to the completion of the neoliberal paradigm shift in the United States and Britain is explained.

The intellectual bond that developed between the Anglo–American governments led by Clinton and Blair is often compared to the one shared by Reagan and Thatcher during the 1980s. By the late 1980s, the Democratic and Labour parties seemed to be in a similar electoral dilemma. Both left-of-center parties had failed to capture executive power for more than a decade. In an effort to remedy this, modernizers in the Labour Party began taking cues from centrists in the Italian Communist Party in developing a more mainstream policy agenda. From these lessons, Neil Kinnock and John Smith engineered a strategy to move the Labour Party into the political center to broaden its appeal among the voting mainstream. By 1990, political strategists and electoral commentators were asking what the Democratic Party could learn from its British counterpart.[6] In a twist of circumstances, according to Desmond King, "within two years the direction of that question was reversed."[7]

Prime Minister Tony Blair and Chancellor of the Exchequer Gordon Brown met with key players in the Clinton campaign in Washington during the transition in 1993. Brown, in particular, frequently met senior economists in the Democratic administration and established critical links that have resulted in remarkable continuities in fiscal as well as monetary policy between the two countries. These critical links were facilitated through such contacts as Ed Balls, the special adviser to the Chancellor. Balls studied under Clinton's Treasury Secretary Larry Summers and Lawrence Katz (who served under Robert Reich in the Department of Labor) while at Harvard. Gordon Brown shared Clinton's belief that economic growth was dependent on increasing the amount of private capital available for investment. To accomplish this, both leaders believed that they needed to commit their governments to adopting fiscally sound policies that would lead to low long-term interest rates, low inflation, and a balanced budget. This could be achieved through disciplined spending policies and modernizing their tax codes in a manner that would augment long-term investment and promote new research and development in emerging sectors. In addition, the Blair government wanted to provide assurance to investors of its commitment to economic growth by adopting central bank independence.

This was a watershed development in British economic policy making, and it represented a major component of the Blair government's neoliberal agenda. In the Fall of 1997, top-level officials in the Clinton administration, such as US Deputy Treasury Secretary Lawrence Summers, Hillary Clinton, and others, met with members in the highest levels of the Blair government to discuss fundamental aspects of economic policy.[8] Gordon Brown's critical decision to grant independence to the Bank of England was made after a series of discussions with the American Federal Reserve Board Chairman (and first among deficit cutters) Alan Greenspan.[9] The Clinton and Blair administrations demonstrated remarkable continuity in their welfare-to-work policies and capital gains tax reforms. Their mutual decision to support policies that held down new social spending in the name of deficit reduction provides strong evidence that the neoliberal paradigm had been "institution-alized" in the fiscal policy apparatus of both countries.

The Clinton administration and deficit reduction

The FY 2000 budget represented a paradigm shift in budgetary policy making in the United States.[10] A revolution occurred in US fiscal policy whereby the discretionary side of the budget was balanced without drawing on entitle-ments. The two sides of the US fiscal budget are composed of the Social Security trust fund, which finances pensions, and everything else. However, although the Social Security trust fund was producing large surpluses in the 1990s, the rest—known as the budget on balance—was in deficit. According to *The Economist*, "[S]ince the trust fund surpluses outweighed the deficits, the overall budget was in surplus."[11] Therefore, most political rhetoric regarding the overall growing budget surplus in the 1990s obscured the difference between the two sides. According to Bob Reichauer, former director of the Congressional Budget Office, in the FY 2000 budget "politicians changed the aim of fiscal policy from balancing the unified budget to balancing the budget without counting on the Social Security surplus."[12] This was a hallmark achievement for deficit cutters, who finally got the overall balanced budget they were seeking.

The Clinton administration's decision to make deficit reduction its highest fiscal priority in place of any investment plan reflected the administration's wholesale acceptance of neoliberal ideas and its unswerving commitment to deficit reduction. The administration pursued fiscal policy strategies that were in direct accordance with monetary goals. Economic stability became the single most important consideration in setting fiscal goals. Clinton set his deficit reduction target of $500 billion over five years in accordance with the specific recommendations made by the Federal Reserve Chairman Alan Greenspan about the expectations of financial markets.

The expectations of financial markets and, more precisely, the bond market came to represent a central concern in Clinton's overall economic strategy.[13] The administration was acutely concerned about the unprecedented gap between short-term and long-term interest rates.[14] According to Paul Pierson, the Clinton administration saw this as "a sign of market skepticism about [the previous government's] handling of the deficit."[15] Clinton and deficit cutters in the administration were specifically concerned about the causal link between the growing public debt and high long-term interest rates.[16] The administration believed that the best way to bring long-term interest rates down was to control growth of the federal deficit.[17] Administration officials and advisers believed that a credible deficit-reduction strategy was desperately needed to ameliorate the problem. According to Bob Woodward, "Clinton felt that the long-term interest rates had been too high for too long. The middle class, he felt, could not improve its condition unless interest rates came down."[18] At the same time, the administration understood that long-term interest rates were a critical concern for both businesses with large debts and people with mortgages.[19] The administration committed itself to an interest rate strategy as its highest fiscal policy goal; Clinton placed it ahead of the spending investment strategy "to grow the economy."[20]

Clinton's core commitment to the deficit reduction issue was visible through his appointments of such deficit "hawks" as Alice Rivlin, Lloyd Bensten, Robert Rubin, Lawrence Summers, and Leon Panetta to key economic policy positions, such as the Office of Management and Budget (OMB), Secretary of the Treasury, and White House Chief of Staff. Clinton adopted the most ambitious deficit targets proposed by the deficit hawks in his cabinet.[21] Having learned from the experiences of the Reagan administration of the dangers of not adopting a clear deficit-reduction policy, Clinton adopted a clear and coherent deficit-reduction strategy from the beginning of his administration. By establishing himself as a devout deficit cutter, Clinton was able to cultivate support among like-minded actors within the policy subsystem, rendering possible the achievement of critical cuts in discretionary spending in a manner that Reagan could not.

Mobilizing the necessary support for major policy change is never a simple matter and is certain to draw political conflict over the appropriateness of contending strategies. Political conflict regarding the deficit reduction issue has been shaped by disagreements among contending coalitions and the competition for institutionalizing core policy beliefs. The Clinton administration found itself embroiled in a conflict involving how much revenue would come from cuts in existing entitlements versus how much would come from new taxes. The administration ultimately pursued cuts in discretionary spending in such areas as housing, transportation, and defense but wanted to protect funding for entitlements, the environment, and education. Paul Pierson brings out that the largest source of new revenues, however, could not be found in discretionary spending but rather in entitlements.[22] The Congressional budget plan strongly differed from the one proposed by the administration in that it sought sharp increases in the premiums for Medicare and Medicaid.

Protecting entitlements was the defining issue in the conflict over deficit reduction strategies between the White House and opponents in Congress. Disagreements revolving around this issue led to two budget impasses, in 1995 and FY 1996.[23] The package that was ultimately enacted reflected most of the administration's initial goals.[24] The Democratic administration eventually came to realize that it would have to draw on the entitlement side of the budget for the necessary savings needed to eliminate the deficit. In that vein, the Clinton administration enacted new taxes on Social Security benefits for affluent retirees, of which almost $50 billion would come from Medicare and Medicaid.[25] Paul Pierson brings out that when "combined with smaller cuts made elsewhere, and reductions in interest payments resulting from the smaller anticipated deficits, however, these changes in entitlements meant that spending cuts would roughly match the tax increases in contributing to a lower deficit while leaving significant funds for the administration's domestic agenda."[26]

The Clinton administration's historic decision to tax Social Security benefits paid to America's wealthiest retirees represented a shift in the Democratic Party's traditional position towards entitlements. This was an unprecedented development as both left- and right-of-center governments alike had up to that point viewed entitlements as a sacred cow that could not be touched. In taxing the Social Security benefits of America's wealthier individuals, the Clinton administration demonstrated that it was even prepared to sacrifice the sacred cow of Social Security to balance the country's budget. This shift in the traditional position of the Democratic leadership regarding the deficit versus entitlements was rooted in the process of policy learning both within the party and the larger policy subsystem.

Explaining the shift in the US fiscal policy subsystem

Policy learning is characterized by enduring alterations in causal beliefs and entails the search for improved mechanisms to attain core values. Policy learning was instrumental in altering the basic precepts and causal assumptions regarding preexisting borrowing and spending patterns and their overall effect on economic growth. Over the last decade, policy makers and academics have had an opportunity to observe and collect empirical data on the effects of deficit spending on the economy.[27] Economists and economic policy makers, such as Martin Feldstein, who had been conducting analyses of fiscal trends based on rational choice models to predict the size of future deficits and their potential effects on economic performance in the 1970s and 1980s, concluded that the budget deficit could have detrimental effects on the economy in the future.[28]

The conflict between tax cutters and deficit cutters largely shaped political competition within the US fiscal policy subsystem in the Reagan era. At the same time, both coalitions were mutually engaged in the neoliberal struggle to dethrone the KWS paradigm. These coalitions were composed of like-minded actors who made up the fiscal policy subsystem. They included, in the United States for example, critical actors in the OMB, the Council of Economic Advisors, the Treasury Department, important advocates in Congress, and important actors in the financial community, experts in academia, and the elite media. From this system of dominant beliefs, the next phase of deficit reduction arose in the 1990s. Figure 4.3 illustrates the intrapartisan coalitions in the US fiscal policy subsystem from Clinton to Reagan.

External shocks facilitate the redistribution of resources that, in turn, can create new opportunities for minority coalitions and impose new constraints on dominant ones. The Balanced Budget and Emergency Control Act, or Gramm–Rudman–Hollings, helped to change fundamentally the fiscal policy

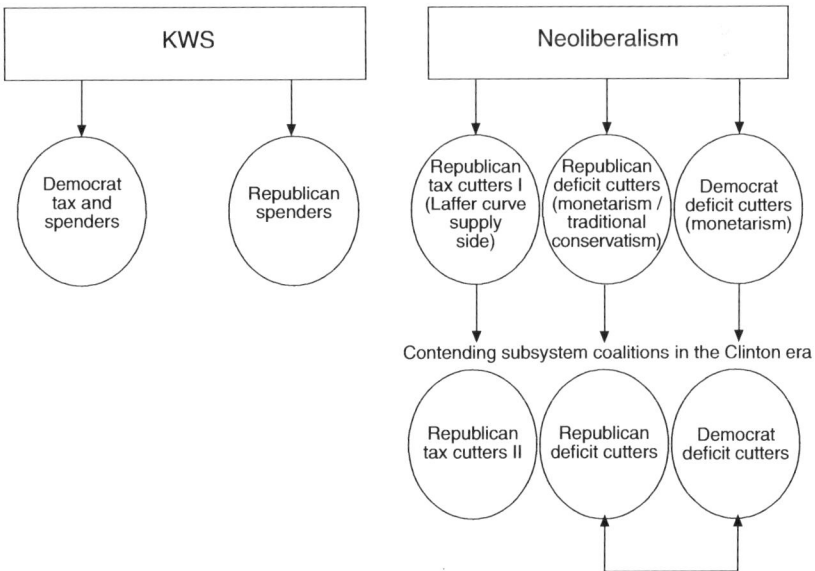

Figure 4.3 Contending subsystem coalitions from the Reagan and Clinton eras compared

subsystem in the United States over the course of almost a generation. As US growth declined while government spending substantially increased, arguments supporting Gramm–Rudman–Hollings began to resonate with larger audiences across partisan lines. The first phase of the deficit reduction initiative in the United States began in the 1980s and was characterized by a targeted criticism of the KWS and the enormous tax-and-spending engine it generated. The second phase of the deficit reform effort reemerged in the policy agendas of the new Democrats led by Clinton. Convinced by the arguments of deficit cutters, Clinton and new Democrats came to believe that fiscal prudence was the best means for encouraging new investment in the private sector and, hence, higher growth overall. In this process, deficit reduction became intrinsically linked with the neoliberal paradigm and its core assumption that excessive government was, at least in part, responsible for economic decline. Although large budget deficits had previously been regarded as an inescapable source of inflation, they were now seen as a major cause of declining savings and investment.[29] The new Democrats began distancing themselves from traditional alliances with organized labor by renouncing the logic of collective wage bargaining, instead embracing monetary and fiscal stability as the highest economic priority.

New Democrats grew increasingly concerned about the effects of deficit spending on long-term interest rates and declining levels of private investment. The effect of high long-term interest rates on the bond market became their highest macroeconomic concern. These developments, coupled with the now obvious shift from manufacturing to service industries, caused policymakers on both sides of the partisan divide to reexamine their policy beliefs. A growing consensus composed of moderates and conservatives belonging to both parties began to view the deficit as a critical economic problem that threatened the growth of productive investment.[30]

The variable of timing was a critical factor to this process. Armed with more than 20 years of empirical data suggesting that large deficits were clearly responsible for raising long-term interest rates, economic instability, disinvestments, and low growth, Alan Greenspan convinced Clinton that a credible and sizable deficit-reduction plan would bring down long-term interest rates.[31] Clinton was further persuaded by Greenspan's argument that a credible deficit-reduction plan was needed to initiate a sustained economic recovery.[32] Clinton ultimately concurred with Greenspan's assessment that without such a plan, another recession would rear its head in less than two years, regardless of any short-term stimulus policy that might be enacted. Although Greenspan helped to refine and validate Clinton's commitment to fiscal discipline, deficit reduction had been a core concern of both Clinton and the centrist DLC going back to 1985. The DLC regarded the deficit and its effect on high long-term interest rates as the main impediment to the creation of new capital investment in crucial sectors of the economy, such as small business, research and development, high-tech, and knowledge-intensive service industries. Capital investment in these emerging sectors was viewed to be critical in promoting the kind of economic growth that was needed to guarantee the long-term solvency of Social Security.[33] Alan Greenpsan, who led Reagan's bipartisan commission to restore the long-term integrity of Social Security in the 1980s, asserted that a dramatic reduction in the size of the deficit was instrumental in this process.[34]

Despite the Clinton administration's initial assertion that a (short-term) government-led investment strategy was required to "jump start the economy" in the early 1990s, the Democrat-led Congress refused to approve it, largely on the grounds that it was fiscally imprudent. The program proposed a stimulus package of $30 billion in spending and tax cuts for investment in infrastructure and job creation that would cover FYs 1993 and 1994.[35] Conservatives on both sides of the partisan fence viewed the program as a ploy to frame new spending as investment and defeated it on that basis. Although the stimulus package was a highly visible part of Clinton's 1992 election campaign, it was not a core policy concern for the Clinton administration. Clinton always intended for the package to be a short-term remedy to boosting employment and economic growth, but it was never meant to replace or jeopardize the core long-term policy goals of balancing the budget that he believed was required for shoring-up Social Security, maintaining stable levels of monetary growth, and bringing down long-term interest rates. The Democrat-led Congress's refusal to support new spending, and the Clinton administration's decision not to press the issue, demonstrated the importance of the budget deficit issue in the political discourse even at that time.

The shift in the importance of deficit reduction from the Reagan period to the Bush–Clinton era was driven by new evidence and growing public awareness. Both Republican and Democratic deficit cutters dramatically reshaped the dimensions of the policy debate by abandoning traditional partisan-based policies and programs and coming together in support of deficit reduction. Republican deficit cutters changed the language regarding their tax reform agenda, from "No new taxes" to "Fair taxes" in an effort to deal with the deficit problem. This development coupled with the Democratic deficit cutters' acceptance of new taxes on entitlements, an area of fiscal policy once thought to be beyond reproach, leveled the political field for bipartisan cooperation and compromise on the deficit reduction issue. These historic concessions enabled deficit cutters on both sides of the partisan fence to come together and create a winning coalition.

The policy priorities of leaders from both parties shifted since the 1980s. In the 1980s, for example, Reagan, a Republican, rallied for major increases in military spending at the expense of expanding the budget deficit. By the early 1990s, Bush, by way of contrast, also a Republican, began making aggressive cuts in military expenditure in an effort to alleviate pressure on the deficit. And counter-intuitively, Clinton, a Democrat, sought to levy taxes on entitlements (specifically in the area of Social Security), institute a major welfare retrenchment initiative, and attack domestic discretionary spending all in the name of deficit reduction. The combined efforts of deficit cutters from both parties facilitated the development of a historic consensus for eliminating the deficit.

By the early 1990s, the fiscal policy subsystem in the United States had shifted since the Reagan era toward neoliberal hegemony. In the 1990s, the discourse had shifted from one dominated by Keynesian tax-and-spenders on one end and tax cutters on the other toward one centered around deficit reduction. The fiscal policy subsystem during the Bush and Clinton eras was, therefore, shaped by the conflict between tax cutters and a new bipartisan coalition of deficit cutters. This new coalition of deficit cutters (which included many Republicans) was willing to abandon secondary aspects of their policy beliefs (such as supporting tax increases) to alleviate deficit spending that had skyrocketed to nearly $300 billion.

Three significant intrapartisan coalitions had evolved by 1992. First, Republican deficit cutters, now a larger voice in the party, had successfully established deficit reduction as the dominant issue in the party. Second, Democratic deficit cutters included a group of neoliberals collectively known as New Democrats led by Tim Roemer (IN), Calvin Dooley (CA), and Jim Moran (VA), and a more conservative group known as "Blue Dog Democrats" led by Gary Condit (CA), Collin Peterson (MN) and John Tanner (TN), as well a number of House members belonging to the DLC-affiliated caucus known as the "Mainstream Forum." By the early 1990s, these neoliberal groups had managed to capture their Party's mainstream agenda under the leadership of Bill Clinton. Third, Republican tax cutters II emerged, composed of a combination of those who saw tax cuts as the main vehicle for restoring private incentive and entrepreneurial initiative as well as those who supported them for reasons of political expediency.

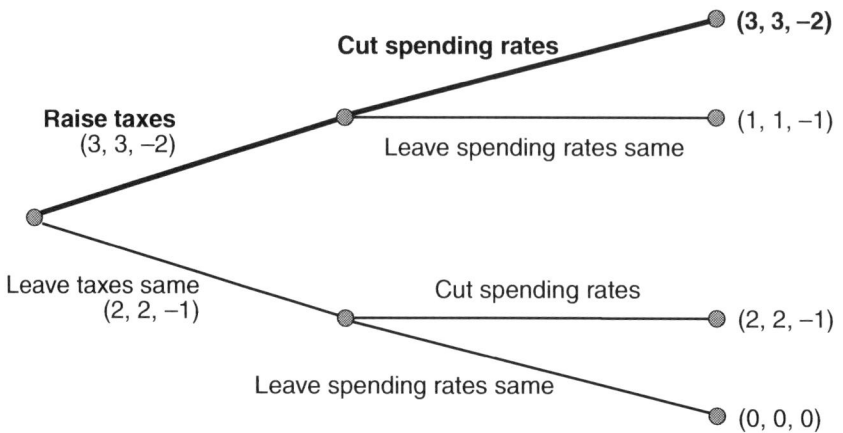

Figure 4.4 Non-cooperative sequential game tree illustrating preference options of significant coalitional partners in fiscal policy subsystem during Clinton era (1990s) (please note that there is no interaction assumed between tax and spending references)

The preference rankings regarding distinct fiscal strategies for the three intrapartisan coalitions are presented using a noncooperative three-player sequential game tree (Figure 4.4). When Clinton and the new Democrats took power in 1993, partisanship initially kept Republican deficit cutters from cooperating with Democratic deficit cutters despite the fact that they shared critical core policy beliefs regarding the need for fiscal prudence. After the Republicans won the House and Senate in the 1994 election, however, Clinton found the Republican deficit cutters far more willing to cooperate with his administration than they had been when they were in the minority. The game tree illustrates that both groups had an incentive to cooperate on the basis of their shared core policy beliefs. We place Republican deficit cutters as Player 1 and Democratic deficit cutters as Player 2. Republican tax cutters II are represented as Player 3. In the changed policy subsystem, the game tree model illustrates that the best scenario for both Republican and Democratic deficit cutters was to pursue spending cuts while actually supporting some increases in taxes. This put them at direct odds with Republican tax cutters II, whose best expected outcome under the changed structure of the fiscal policy subsystem could only be "Leave taxes the same." The equilibrium path for the players in this game is indicated by large bold type in the figure. The model illustrates that the Nash solution— "raise taxes" and "cut spending"—wins.

Building coalitional support for fiscal policy change under Clinton: the role of heresthetics

Bringing about major shifts in policy requires building a new coalitional majority through political framing known as *heresthetics*. Building sufficient coalitional support for major budgetary reform would require a leader who not only possessed a deep core commitment to fiscal discipline but could successfully build a bipartisan consensus within the *Washington establishment* that would support tighter budget spending. Having learned from Reagan's experience regarding the importance of establishing a clear and resolute commitment to the deficit reduction cause early on, President Clinton presented a line-by-line deficit reduction plan to the nation less than a month after taking office.[36] The newly elected president put his deficit-reduction agenda even ahead of the economic stimulus package to jump start the economy for which he had rallied throughout the 1992 campaign.[37]

Clinton was able to cultivate support within a new breed of deficit cutters.[38] His ability to do so was rooted in heresthetics. He helped to lead a new coalition that included not only many of the traditional deficit cutters from the previous decade (many of them moderate Republicans) but a growing group of deficit-reduction advocates belonging to the new left of center as well.[39] As brought out earlier, the Clinton administration was remarkably successful in reframing the issue of deficit reduction from one shaped by the "politics of blame avoidance" to one of "political credit claiming."[40] By removing the stigma of "ruthless" previously associated with fiscal austerity, Clinton was able to launch an aggressive offensive against the deficit in a manner that proved to be politically acceptable to many belonging to the left of center. After nearly a decade and a half of struggling to bring awareness to the cause of deficit reduction, deficit cutters had at long last brought the issue to the top of the policy agenda.

The coalition included a critical middle class-business consensus that incorporated the support of staunch deficit cutters on both sides of the political fence. According to Desmond King, "[Clinton's] tough line on welfare was crucial in establishing this middle class electoral base: it reassured voters that personal income tax levels would not be threatened by social budgets."[41] When Bill Clinton announced his candidacy for president in 1991, the *New York Times* described his speech as "relentlessly focusing on the middle-class."[42] Having committed his administration to a balanced budget, Clinton was able to build support among a critical group of disenchanted Republican voters who agreed with Ross Perot on the urgency of bringing down deficit spending.[43] Clinton pollster and political strategist Stanley Greenberg concisely explains the importance of attracting middle-class Perot voters in support for the administration's neoliberal agenda.[44] In a national survey of Perot voters conducted by the DLC, those voters older than 30 had largely voted Republican in recent elections.[45] Greenberg and his team found "that nearly three quarters (73 percent) of voters older than fifty had voted for either Reagan or Bush; and for those age thirty to fifty, a very respectable two-thirds (67 percent) had voted for one or the other. Among all Perot voters, 62 percent voted for Reagan at least once, and 62 percent voted for Bush in 1988."[46] According to Greenberg, Clinton's fiscal agenda strongly appealed to this critical but disillusioned group by demonstrating that he shared their beliefs in the market as the "best engine for prosperity."[47] Greenberg further brings out that Clinton was committed to a set of economic beliefs that "first and foremost meant a commitment to economic growth, expanding investments in emerging technologies, as well as providing more incentives to invest by US companies in their own country."[48]

The election of a Republican majority to Congress in 1994 marked a critical juncture in the deficit-reduction effort—albeit for a very different set of reasons than are normally assumed. Bob Woodward notes that on entering office, Al Gore and the new president agreed to "confidentially sound out" Republican deficit hawks in the Senate and House in an effort to build a bipartisan agreement on a Social Security cost-of-living adjustment freeze to alleviate pressure on the budget.[49] The vice-president found that "not one would agree to even discuss it."[50] With the election of a Republican majority to the US Congress in 1994, however, the deficit reduction cause drew the support of monetarists and traditional conservatives. Having gained control of both houses of Congress, Republican Party deficit hawks, such as Ways and Means Chairman John Kasich (who asserted that "there is no compromise with a balanced budget") and Senate Budget Committee Chairman Pete Domenici, appeared more willing to work with the Clinton administration on the deficit-reduction issue.[51] Even such Republican tax cutters as Dick Armey began championing deficit reduction as a weapon in the enduring assault against the redistributive policy apparatus. Of course, tax cutters such as Armey were never prepared to support tax increases for the cause of deficit reduction.

New Democrats, along with members affiliated with the Mainstream Forum and the Blue Dog Democrats cooperated with moderate Republicans belonging to groups such as the Tuesday Lunch Bunch, led by Fred Upton (R-MI), Nancy Johnson (R-CT), Mike Castle (R-DE), and Christopher Shays (R-CT) and the Mainstream Conservative Alliance headed by W.J. Tauzin (R-LA), in bringing about critical budget compromises.[53] In cooperation with their allies in the Senate, such as John Breaux (D-LA) and Senator John H. Chafee (R-RI), who headed the bipartisan centrist coalition, House deficit cutters worked with the Clinton administration in bringing about a deficit reduction compromise that represented an "effective break on new social spending" from the Reagan, Bush, and Clinton administrations.[54]

The Blair government and deficit reduction

The failure of demand-management strategies to ameliorate the problems associated with stagflation, deindustrialization, and the oil shocks in the 1960s, 1970s, and 1980s provided strong empirical evidence that traditional Keynesian remedies were no longer effective. Members of the ideological right and left of center in Britain began reexamining the fundamental axioms and precepts of the KWS paradigm and began asking critical questions about the proper scope of government in the economy. The currency crisis that led to International Monetary Fund (IMF) intervention in 1976 in Britain, for example, motivated modernizers in the Labour Party to begin considering alternative (neoliberal) economic fiscal strategies.[55] According to Nick Ellison, "[T]he result so far as social policy was concerned, was that Labour began to recognize just how impossible it was to combine economic growth with commitments to ever-increasing social spending."[56] Modernizers in the Labour Party began to realize the limitations of the state in being able to control broader structural changes that were taking place in the economy. The decline in manufacturing sectors and subsequent increases in service-sector employment represented major external shocks that led to unacceptably high levels of structural unemployment. These experiences caused modernizers to emphasize economic stability over wealth redistribution as the best means for promoting social prosperity.[57]

Adopting neoliberal strategies entailed fundamentally altering the Labour Party's core macroeconomic policy beliefs. In 1997, the newly elected government vowed not to seek additional spending for health, education, and social security and asserted that welfare reform could be implemented within existing fiscal means.[58] Labour's fiscal plans disallowed any increases in social spending and specifically prohibited any income tax rate hikes for that purpose. This is true except for the one-off "windfall tax" on privatized utilities that would go specifically to pay for the new welfare-to-work program, or *workfare*, based on the US model.[59] Stephen Driver and Luke Martell bring out that "in health, education, and social security, extra funding would come from 'efficiency savings' and from the phasing out of Conservative programs, or from money sitting in local authority bank accounts as in the case of housing (which would in fact raise public expenditure)."[60]

The neoliberal paradigm shift in the Labour Party was strongly reinforced by the "new Democrat Party" platform and the electoral victory of Bill Clinton in 1992.[61] Clinton's election and the winning appeal of the "Third-Way" economic agenda inspired the new left in Britain to pursue neoliberal policy goals with a new electoral confidence.[62] Tony Blair and other Labour modernizers were encouraged by the success of the DLC and its ability to reinvigorate the left of center after so many years of Republican control of the White House.[63]

Labour modernizers were particularly impressed by the DLC's ability to steer the Democratic Party toward a neoliberal course.[64] Blair and his colleagues understood that the electoral success of new Labour in the 1997 general election depended on acquiring the support of new constituencies. Following the lead of Clinton and the new Democrats, Blair and the modernizers sought to build credibility among Britain's business community, known as the (financial) *City*, and the country's middle class, known as *Middle England*.[65] According to Driver and Martell, "Middle Englanders were Thatcherites in the 1980s precisely because Thatcherism spoke their language —ownership, opportunity, as opposed to equality and state control."[66]

The developments just described led new Democrats and Labour modernizers to adopt a common set of ideas.[67] Shared ideas between the two governments stemmed from a common intellectual connection that was evident at the highest levels of their economic policy-making structures. Chancellor of the Exchequer Gordon Brown and his closest adviser, Ed Balls, shared a common Harvard background. As brought out earlier, Balls studied under both Lawrence Summers and Lawrence Katz.[68] The three men coauthored an academic paper that analyzed British unemployment by region and skill. They concluded that long-term unemployment was largely the result of "skill mismatches and a loss of the culture of work ..."[69] Both the Clinton and Blair governments' welfare reform strategies were forged in accordance with this basic logic.[70] The adoption of similar policy beliefs by key personnel in the Clinton and Blair governments provides important causal insights in explaining their similar policy strategies.

Consistent with its conservative predecessors, the Blair government sought to help to reinvigorate Britain's economy through neoliberal strategies aimed at empowering an entrepreneur-driven enterprise culture. This was based on the belief in the supremacy of markets for generating societal wealth. Blair and the modernizers believed that well-functioning markets, which are themselves focused on promoting individual private initiative, are necessary to the viability of a modern economy. Therefore, they argued that the most essential task for modern governments is to help to create an economic climate that maximizes entrepreneurial energies. As did Clinton, Blair believed that this could be achieved only by rigorously adhering to a strategy of fiscal and monetary prudence.[71] Investors and middle-class interests began to link the "boom–bust" business cycles of the 1980s and 1990s to the ineffectual fiscal and monetary strategies pursued by the Tories when they held power in those years. Specifically, these groups were highly sensitive to the consequences of rampant inflation that they came to believe stemmed from fiscal and monetary imprudence. As a result, the first major policy innovation of the Blair government after the election of 1997 was to grant the Monetary Policy Committee full operational independence in setting short-term interest rates. Although revolutionary, the Bank of England was still not as independent as the US or German central banks as the government retained the prerogative of setting monetary goals—setting the inflation rate. On the fiscal side, the Blair government adopted the "Golden Rule" of public spending that prohibited new borrowing to pay for new social spending. The Chancellor also enacted *the sustainable investment rule*, in which the ratio of public debt to national income was to be set at a "stable and prudent" level. The Treasury established that the public debt rate must not exceed 40 percent of GDP. In addition, the government enacted a *central spending review* and *departmental reviews*, which were later converted to the *1998 Comprehensive Spending Review* and the *2000 Spending Review* to promote the cause of fiscal responsibility and efficiency.

In the 1995 Mais Lecture, Blair asserted that Britain needed to enhance its global competitiveness by adopting a tough and coherent macroeconomic framework governing the country's tax and spending practices. Following this logic, the Blair government instituted a rules-based approach governing fiscal policy that put limits on new spending and taxation. It established new fiscal goals governing macroeconomic policy and sought to direct public spending toward neglected areas with potentially high economic returns.[72] It further called for reform in the area of taxation to broaden the tax base as well as to cut marginal tax rates to provide incentives for investors and job seekers.[73]

In 1998, the Blair government institutionalized the basic principles established in the Mais lecture by adopting the *Code for Fiscal Stability*. The Code required that all budget measures adopted by the Treasury be consistent with long-term government objectives. The Code, therefore, institutionalized five principles of fiscal management: transparency, stability, responsibility, fairness, and efficiency. To render the fiscal policy process more transparent and deliberative, the Code required the Treasury to present a consultative pre-budget report, or green budget, that would outline any significant proposal for changes in fiscal policy at least three months in advance of the final budget.[74] In addition, the Treasury had to publish a *financial statement* as well as its overall *economic fiscal strategy* outlining the long-term spending targets and expected borrowing requirements (public sector borrowing requirement, or PSBR) prior to the formal adoption of any policy itself.[75] The National Audit Office was also required to review and publish a *debt management report* detailing the structure of government borrowing as well as the cost of government debt.[76] Moreover, the Code mandated that public borrowing be used only to finance investment and specifically forbade additional borrowing for new spending.[77]

Blair and the modernizers believed that governments had to hold down spending as a fiscal requisite for promoting overall economic stability.[78] The government sought to maximize investor confidence in the City of London's volatile financial markets by adhering to the spending limits of their Tory predecessors rather than seeking additional revenues through increased borrowing and/or taxation.[79] As a result of new Labour's prudence, public spending in its first two years totaled £2 billion less than the spending plans outlined by its Tory predecessors. Within two years of taking office, the Blair government delivered a balanced budget to the British people. Within its first year in power, new Labour reduced Britain's national deficit from £28 billion to £9 billion.[80] In the budget for 1999–2000, the Chancellor presented a budget surplus of £4 billion that was expected to yield a total surplus for the next five years coming to £34 billion.[81]

The elimination of Britain's PSBR can be directly attributed to cuts in discretionary spending, higher government receipts provided by a resurgent economy.[82] In keeping with its promise to adhere to the spending limits of its Tory predecessors, the Blair government financed additional spending on education and health through the use of the contingency fund, extra revenue generated from the (one-time) windfall tax, and the reallocation of lottery and defense department moneys.[83]

The fiscal policy followed by the Blair government began a trend that virtually guaranteed a balanced budget for the next several years.[84] This was a remarkable achievement in light of the fact that New Labour reversed spending trends that had been responsible for creating substantial deficits over the previous six years.[85] Low inflation, coupled with a growth rate of 2.5 percent, generated greater tax revenues than were initially projected. This, of course, contributed to the impressive decline in the deficit. Naturally, less borrowing meant a reduction in funds having to be spent on interest on the total national debt.

On the monetary side of economic policy, the Blair government was equally committed to neoliberalism. Immediately on taking power in May 1997, the Blair government established a 2.5 percent inflation target (with leeway for half a percent movement in either direction) in an effort to provide an environment of economic stability that would encourage increased growth and productivity.[86] In so doing, New Labour embraced the budgetary goals first proposed under the conservative leadership of Geoffrey Howe and Nigel Lawson amounting to a wholesale shift in economic policy strategies from those advocated under traditional Labour approaches.[87] The Blair government ceded operational authority to the Bank of England to set the national interest rates to assure investors in the City of its whole-hearted commitment to promoting monetary stability.[88]

Blair's macroeconomic policies have inspired confidence among business and consumers alike. Adair Turner, the director general of the Confederation of British Industry, lauded Blair's first major budget in March 1998 for its prudent approach to public spending.[89] The British Chambers of Commerce, which represents smaller companies, announced, "this is a valuable budget for enterprise and employment. It is both prudent and positive."[90] The Blair government acted vigorously to cut public spending and made the bold leap to grant independence to the Bank of England, which immediately raised interest rates to control inflation. Business confidence grew further when the Blair government formally renounced the practice of short-term wage bargaining. In his budget speech of March 17, 1998, Brown issued a warning to employees to exercise restraint so as not to endanger Britain's growth rate that he feared would drop from 2.5 to two percent "if wage bargaining proceeds in the same short-termist way as in the past ..."[91]

British policy makers believed that slow French and German economic recoveries from the recession of the early 1990s stemmed from their *dirigiste* economic orientations, whereas Britain's liberal political-economic system and relatively flexible labor markets were contributory factors in facilitating its relatively swift recovery.[92] Policy makers in the Treasury believed that their adherence to a neoliberal framework afforded them greater flexibility in coping with economic adjustment as compared to their European counter-parts, who characteristically favor more *dirigiste* solutions. This reinforced the Blair government's belief in neoliberalism.

Notwithstanding the importance of a resurgent economy in producing unexpectedly high tax revenues, prudent fiscal policies implemented by the Blair government were essential in eliminating Britain's PSBR. The success of the Blair government in achieving a balanced budget is deeply related to the role of ideas and coalitions in reshaping the fiscal policy subsystem. By the mid-1990s, Labour modernizers, who may be termed *Labour deficit cutters*, had become the dominant voice within the party and had successfully established deficit reduction and fiscal prudence as the central issues within it. What separated Labour Party deficit cutters from Tory Party deficit cutters was their level of commitment to monetarist principles and prescriptions. Whereas Tory deficit cutters made critical strides in the process toward infusing monetarist directives into the budget-making process through the *medium term financial strategy*, which placed fiscal goals subordinate to monetary imperatives, the Bank of England nonetheless remained under the control of the government. Policy elites and service-oriented industries and investors grew increasingly concerned over Britain's waning international competitiveness in the 1990s. These groups applied considerable political pressure that helped to produce a shift in the dimensions of the neoliberal policy discourse within the fiscal policy subsystem from one centered around cutting taxes and spending to one focused on cutting spending and monetary independence. Modernizers believed that controlling inflation, through spending reduction and the depoliticization of Britain's monetary policy, would create the best economic environment for private investment and, hence, economic growth. In following this course, Blair and the modernizers adhered to a more strict application of monetarism than did Thatcher and the other Tory deficit cutters.

In the Thatcher era, political conflict in the fiscal policy subsystem was focused on the struggle over whether to "cut spending" or "leave spending the same" on one side and "cut taxes" or "leave taxes the same" on the other. In the late 1990s, the fiscal policy subsystem was reshaped in a way that became focused on whether to "cut spending" or "leave spending the same" on one side and "promote central bank independence" or "maintain central bank dependence" on the other. Under the changed fiscal policy subsystem, four significant intrapartisan coalitions emerged by the mid-to-late 1990s. They are Labour deficit cutters, Labour tax-and-spenders, Tory deficit cutters, and Tory spenders. Political competition among these four intrapartisan coalitions was structured quite differently from that in the United States. It was mainly shaped by political competition between Tory deficit cutters and Labour Party deficit cutters (who were mostly Labour modernizers). Conflict among the coalitions involved the struggle to win the support of Britain's financial business sector and the middle class. This meant first and foremost being able to implement policies consistent with fiscal prudence and a balanced budget. After 18 years of continuous Conservative governments led by Thatcher and Major, the Tory Party had failed to complete the neoliberal agendas it had proposed. Simply stated, the Tories had lost their credibility as being the party of fiscal prudence and, hence, the support of much of Britain's financial business sector and the middle classes. Figure 4.5 illustrates the intrapartisan coalitions in the British fiscal policy subsystem from Thatcher to Blair.

The preference rankings regarding the distinct fiscal strategies for the four intrapartisan coalitions are presented using a noncooperative three-player sequential game tree in Figure 4.6. We place Labour deficit cutters as the category of Player 1; Labour tax-and-spenders as well as Tory spenders are placed in the category of Player 2; and Tory deficit cutters are placed as Player 3. In the changed policy subsystem, the game tree model illustrates that the best scenario for deficit cutters, now majority players, was to "cut spending" and adopt "central bank independence." As "absolute majority players," they faced no formidable competition from other coalition competitors. As such, this strategy represents the unique Nash solution. In an ever-

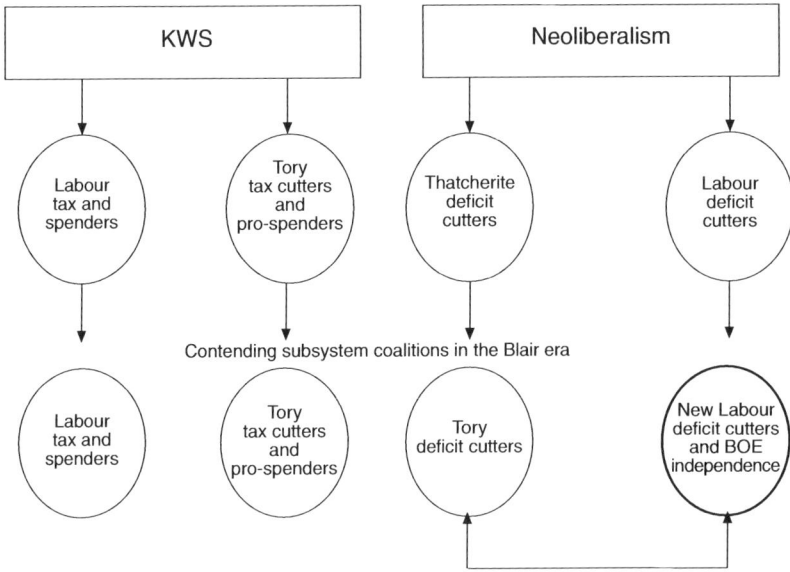

Figure 4.5 Contending subsystem coalitions from the Thatcher and Blair eras compared

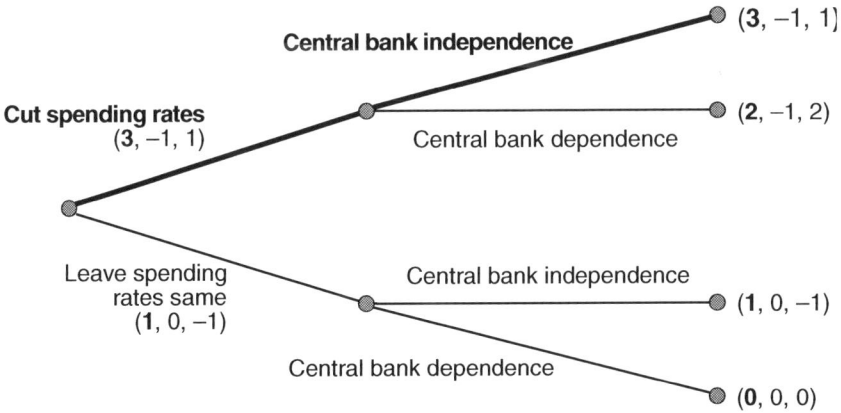

Figure 4.6 Non-cooperative sequential game tree illustrating preference options of significant coalitional partners in fiscal policy subsystem during Blair era (late 1990s) (numbers in bold indicate major player)

growing competitive economic environment, both business investors and middle-class consumers, who had grown extremely sensitive to the consequences of hyperinflation, had become highly supportive of the proposition of a more coherent and "apoliticized" domestic monetary regime. Thus, there was high political support for central bank independence in setting interest rates, as business interests and middle-class voters had become convinced that this would best ensure monetary stability.

Role of heresthetics in facilitating deficit reduction under Blair

As brought out in Chapter 3, Thatcher found putting an end to deficit spending to be an extremely difficult thing to achieve given the resistance from voters and many politicians who opposed cuts in politically popular public programs and benefits. Eliminating Britain's deficit would require a leadership that was able to build a broad consensus among Treasury officials, spending ministers, politicians, voters, business groups, labor unions, and government agencies by convincing them to embrace balanced budgets as a top government priority. Policy learning was, therefore, critical to Blair's success in building broad coalitional support for proposed spending control initiatives. Labour Party modernizers were faced with the challenge of convincing members within their own party, many of whom were former Keynesians themselves, to adopt neoliberal strategies directed at dismantling the KWS. Faith in government-led redistribution had begun to wane over time in response to specific experiences and lessons inferred from them.

The traditional (KWS) macroeconomic policy beliefs held by old Labour were severely challenged in the mid-1970s.[93] Facing a balance-of-payments crisis and the inability to meet the repayment of short-term credit, the Chancellor of the Exchequer, Denis Healey, was forced to apply for a $3.9 billion bailout from the IMF.[94] As it was the largest loan ever extended to any country up until that time, Healey's application was viewed as an admission that there were serious weaknesses in the Labour government's economic management strategies and its adherence to KWS core assumptions.[95] Conditions of the IMF loan required cuts in public spending to the tune of £1 billion in 1977–8 and £1.5 billion in 1978–9.[96]

After almost two decades, both Thatcher and Major proved unable to reduce sufficiently the size of state expenditure and restore private incentives in a manner that would enable Britain to regain its global competitive edge. Simon Lee brings out that "from 1979–97 UK annual growth had averaged only 2.1 percent, well below its post-war trend of 2.4 percent, while government spending had risen by an average of 1.7 percent and total taxation by 1.8 percent. As a consequence, public spending which in 1978–9 consumed 44.9 percent of GDP was only reduced to 41.2 percent of GDP by the final year of the Major government."[97]

Pointing to weaknesses in privatization and deregulation schemes that covered areas from labor market policy to public utilities, inept monetary policies, and their inability to eliminate Britain's PSBR, Labour moderizers accused the Thatcher–Major governments of creating boom–bust political economic business cycles. In the period after the stock market crash in the Fall of 1987, the Thatcher government relaxed fiscal policy to spur growth and generate revenues.[98] By the early 1990s, however, Britain was experiencing one of the severest recessions in 50 years. Poor growth in those years led to "a massive deterioration of the public finances that led to a public sector deficit of 7.8 percent of GDP in 1992–3 and 46 billion pounds in 1993–4, amounting to a fiscal error of almost £50 billion."[99] In response to this, the Major government "had little choice but to increase taxes by nearly one percent of GDP in 1994–5 and more than twice that in 1995–6 and 1996–7."[100] The consequence of these developments caused the Tory Party ultimately to lose the support of Britain's business and middle classes.

Having learned from the failures of his predecessors, Blair understood that his neoliberal fiscal agenda would have to win the confidence of the City's financial markets were it to be successfully implemented. To accomplish this, the Blair government instituted reforms that rendered the macroeconomic policy process more deliberative and transparent in an effort to assure both domestic and international investors of its commitment to fiscal discipline. The Blair government promoted its macroeconomic policy agenda through heavy coordination with critical subsystem actors in the Treasury, spending departments, cabinet committees, quangos, task forces, business groups, and many others. In addition, it established at least 318 task forces to advise and support ministers so as to facilitate greater coordination both within and among central government departments. These task forces created a new appointed or nominated elite, disproportionately composed of producer interests (71 percent) as compared to consumer interests (15 percent).[101]

The 1998 and 2000 spending reviews and the public service agreements were instituted to bring greater coordination to the budget process.[102] The Central Spending Review assesses the most efficient use of resources so as to eliminate waste and inefficiency. The Comprehensive Spending Review (CSR) replaced the annual Public Expenditure Survey with a three-year resolution that established departmental spending limits.[103] This allowed departments to design policy over the long term and enabled the Prime Minister's office to adopt a more strategic approach to public spending. Public service agreements were set up to facilitate greater coordination between each of the spending departments and the Treasury and established new efficiency and effectiveness targets.[104] Service delivery agreements were added in the July 2000 spending review that outlined specific strategies for maximizing existing expenditures.[105] Lee illuminates that this entailed integrating "policy design and resource allocation for England and its regions at the central government level notably through the creation of a series of new units within the Cabinet Office, notably through the Social Exclusion Unit and Performance Innovation Unit (PIU)."[106]

Through its effort to bring greater coordination among actors in the economic policy subsystem, the Blair government has been remarkably successful in (1) building broad intrapartisan support for its spending policies and (2) bringing greater coherence and formality to the policy process itself. In opening the policy debate to a broad array of affected actors, and thereby widening subsystem participation in the process of policy design and implementation through spending reviews, green budgets, and so on, the Blair government was able to build a consensus for major fiscal change.

Tax reform under President Clinton and Prime Minister Blair

The Clinton and Blair administrations exhibited remarkable parallels in their tax reform initiatives that stem from a shared set of core and secondary policy beliefs. Tax strategies adopted by the Clinton and Blair governments were pursued in accordance with their primary deficit-reduction goals, which were meant to bolster opportunities for business and the middle class.[107] Their tax policies were designed to provide relief for corporations, to institute or expand earned income tax credits, and to provide tax cuts for capital gains. Clinton and Blair introduced sweeping changes in the tax structure designed to generate investment in new technologies, research and development, and start-up companies that created incentives for venture capitalists.[108]

Gordon Brown's first minor budget as Chancellor in July of 1997 focused first and foremost on reforming Britain's corporate tax system, which he and his advisers thought did not properly reward long-term investment.[109] In November of 1997, Brown announced that the Treasury would begin serious deliberations regarding the introduction of a working families tax credit to aid the working poor; it was directly modeled after the US earned income tax credit (EITC).[110] Clinton's expansion of the EITC as a means of encouraging investment in human capital heavily influenced Brown's tax reform strategy targeting the UK's socially excluded.[111] Larry Katz, former chief economist in the Labor Department and a former professor of the Chancellor's closest adviser, Ed Balls, wrote a paper with Jeffrey Liebman for the new Blair government on America's experience with the EITC.[112]

Tax reform in the Clinton era: partisan convergence in broad tax policy goals

The election of 1994, and the ascendancy of the Republican majority in the House and Senate marked an important juncture in the tax reform debate in the United States. The economic policies outlined in the Contract with America sought a balanced budget amendment to the Constitution; a variety of tax relief from capital gains to families; and sweeping reforms in the welfare system. Conflicts between the president and Congress over contending budget proposals led to two government shutdowns before Congress and the president reached a compromise in April 1996.[113]

In FY 1995, a bipartisan compromise among the administration and other deficit cutters in the Republican Party in Congress (and particularly in the Senate) was reached on a modest middle-class tax cut. While tax cutters and deficit cutters in the Republican Party jointly embraced the overall logic of pursuing low deficits and low taxes, they were divided over which issue was in need of the greatest attention. The two coalitions were sharply divided over the need and desirability of instituting targeted tax cuts versus across-the-board tax cuts. This conflict reflected the struggle over their distinct core policy values. The conflict between the two groups was over the nature and amount of the tax cuts that each proposed.

The conflict between deficit cutters and tax cutters in the Republican Party was heightened in the 1996 budget go-around. This was especially true in the Senate as ardent tax cutters, such as Trent Lott (R-MS), were sharply divided against deficit cutters, such as Pete Domenici (R-NM).[114] As the deficit moved to the forefront of the American political agenda, it was clear that any proposed tax cut would have to be accompanied by similar reductions in spending. This meant that the larger the tax cut, the deeper the spending reductions would have to be to offset it. The Clinton administration, therefore, would not support much more than a limited tax cut for middle-income families (those earning less than $75,000 a year).[115] The president's plan proposed $105 billion in tax cuts over seven years; the breaks would be targeted at middle-income and lower-income families.[116] His proposal included a $500-per-child credit for children younger than 13 and for families earning up to $65,000.[117] It also provided a deduction for tuition and fees up to $10,000 a year for college and graduate school.[118]

Tax cutters in the House proposed and mobilized support for $353 billion in tax cuts aimed at families and businesses. It proposed a $500-per-child tax credit to families earning up to $200,000 and a reduction in individual and corporate capital gains taxes and phased out the corporate alternative minimum tax.[119] The Senate plan, by contrast, did not call for any additional tax cuts until it could be assured of a balanced budget by 2002. Once it was balanced, deficit cutters in the Senate reasoned, Congress could then enact as much as $170 billion in tax cuts over seven years.[120]

Clearly, the late 1990s were strikingly different from the decade prior when Reagan made reducing marginal tax rates the single most important fiscal priority of his administration. By the late 1980s, however, the tax reform issue was overshadowed by growing concerns over instability caused by the enormous growth in the size of the public debt. Budget rules, enacted in 1990 under the Ominibus Reconciliation Bill, required that tax cuts be funded within existing means. Since then, efforts to reduce taxes characteristically have engendered a fight over which programs will be eliminated or which taxes will have to be raised to offset it. According to Michael Meeropol, "though the so-called Reagan revolution was only partially successful in changing policy and though the effects it had on the economy have been the subject of hot dispute, with the hindsight of history it is clear that those initial efforts finally met success in the bipartisanship before and after the presidential election of 1996."[121] Economic policy makers no longer regard traditional Keynesian tax-and-spending policies as legitimate devices for reducing unemployment.[122] Rather, the Federal Reserve System was effectively granted total authority to control both inflation and unemployment. This development provides strong evidence of neoliberal hegemony governing tax policy at that time.[123]

Clinton followed George H. Bush in raising taxes on wealthy taxpayers as part of the effort to balance the budget. Both Bush and Clinton had acted in accordance with the reigning principles established by Gramm–Rudman–Hollings and the Omnibus Reconciliation Act of 1990. In addition, Clinton expanded the EITC, which reduced the tax liability of the 45 percent of taxpayers who earned less than $30,000 a year.[124] During the 1992 campaign, Clinton announced that, if elected, he would pay for a middle-class and lower-class tax cut by raising taxes on America's wealthiest earners.

The EITC initially sought to reduce taxes on working individuals with dependent children. When it was ultimately implemented, however, the expansion led to a tax cut for every wage earner making less than $30,000 a year. In addition, Clinton sought to increase the top marginal income tax rate from 31 to 36 percent, with an additional 10 percent surcharge for taxpayers earning more than $250,000 of taxable income.[125] He proposed increasing the percentage of Social Security payments subject to taxes for retired couples with incomes higher than $32,000 a year. According to Meeropol, when taken together, these changes ended up increasing the tax burden on the top 20 percent of taxpayers.[126]

Preexisting tensions between tax cutters and deficit cutters across partisan lines were accentuated during the political struggle over the FY 2000 budget in the House and Senate regarding the size and scope of the proposed tax cuts. Tax cutters, such as House Ways and Means Chairman Bill Archer (R-TX), the lead House tax writer, stated that they wanted all the unanticipated surplus of FY Budget 2000 to be applied to an even larger tax cut than Republicans had initially planned. Acting in accord with Democratic deficit cutters, such Republican deficit cutters as Budget Committee Chairmen Rep. John R. Kasich (R-OH) and Sen. Pete Domenici (R-NM) refused to commit to further tax cuts until a viable solution was reached for shoring up Social Security and Medicare.

The Clinton administration insisted that tax cuts not jeopardize the established deficit reduction targets. Naturally, disputes arose between ardent tax cutters in Congress and the administration (and other deficit cutters) over the size and structure of the tax cuts. Clinton's plan targeted middle-income earners. He later proposed a "middle-class bill of rights" in the face of a host of tax cut proposals initiated by members of Congress.[127] Although there had been two shutdowns of the federal government and a series of heated debates between the president and ardent tax cutters in Congress to that point, the contending coalitions were simply arguing over the method of achieving a policy on which they were all in general agreement. The Administration sought to pay for its tax cut proposal by making substantial spending cuts in the Department of Urban Housing and Development (HUD), the Department of Energy, the Department of Transportation, the General Services Administration, and the Office of Personnel Management.[128]

Business and capital gains tax reforms

Within less than a year after the 1996 election, disproportionate majorities in both houses passed a budget and a tax agreement that had been designed jointly by the Clinton administration and the Republican majority in Congress.[129] The cuts represented a breakthrough compromise between the Clinton administration and tax cutters in the Republican-led House. This "historic compromise" paved the way for similar bipartisan budget agreements in the later years.[130]

The sustained economic boom largely facilitated these historic tax compromises in 1996 and 1997. Economic prosperity rendered the amount of spending reductions necessary to achieve a balanced budget by 2002 much smaller than when Congress had passed a bill with the same goal in 1995. According to Meeropol, "[T]he overall result of this agreement was to complete a revolution in economic policy making."[131] With the signing of the budget and tax bills in August 1997, the neoliberal convergence was completed. Deficit reduction and tax reform became tangible realities that were supported by a broad membership in both political parties and both the legislative and executive branches of government.[132] These tax reforms represent a successful assault on one of the main redistributive instruments of the KWS that had been legitimized from the Great Depression to the 1970s.[133]

The 1997 US budget marked a critical juncture for both business and capital gains tax relief. Clinton and Congress jointly supported a package of tax cuts for business of more than $10 billion over five years and $20 billion over 10 years.[134] The law also included two significant family tax cuts: a $5,000 tax credit to help to offset the cost of adoption and a $2,000 tax-deferred individual retirement account for nonworking spouses.[135] Interestingly, efforts to cut business taxes had their origins in the tax cut plan proposed in the Republican's Contract with America. In fact, a majority of the tax cuts benefited big business and wealthy workers by allowing pension plans to become more generous. The business tax cut that was ultimately passed benefited business interests across all sectors, including small businesses, restaurant delivery, companies that offered defined contribution plans (i.e., 401 K plans), and multinational high-technology firms.[136] The 1997 tax bill ended up providing cuts for some of the largest companies in the United

States, such as Hewlett-Packard, Johnson and Johnson, Microsoft, and Domino's Pizza.[137]

The FY 1998 budget yielded a $98 billion tax cut package that provided further relief for capital gains and estate taxes. Bipartisan support was expected from the beginning as administration officials sent a clear message that they were prepared to bargain with tax cutters in Congress. This was affirmed when Treasury Secretary Lawrence Summers formally announced, "There is the desire to cooperate ... I think there is the prospect for finding common ground."[138] Clinton's tax package targeted $88 billion of the $98 billion tax cut toward families earning less than $100,000 a year.[139] The three largest cuts included a $500-per-child tax credit, a $10,000 tax reduction, and a $1,500 tax credit for post-secondary school education. It also included an expansion of IRAs for couples with taxable incomes up to $100,000 a year.[140] The remaining $10 billion in tax reductions were earmarked for business investment in poor communities, augmenting existing business tax credits, deductions for research, and expanding the capital gains tax cut. Former Reagan appointee William Niskanen expressed publicly that the Clinton administration's budget "is looking very much like a [President George] Bush tax proposal ... It looks like a Republican tax cut but a little smaller."[141] Both plans targeted the largest portions of the tax cut at middle-income workers, sought to expand IRAs, and entailed some kind of capital gains tax cut.

Tax reform under the new left in Britain: partisan convergence in broad tax policy goals

In its first major budget (March of 1998), the Blair government enacted the "working families tax credit," which sought to cover more people than the family credit initiated under the previous Tory government.[142] It provided a guaranteed weekly income of £180 for a family with full-time wage earners and instituted cuts in employees national insurance contributions and made them adjustable so that less was charged for low-paid workers and more for the highly paid.[143] The new government left the tax breaks for upper-income earners virtually intact, preserved tax relief for mortgage interest payments, and continued to protect money in special share schemes by keeping them tax-free.[144]

Promoting enterprise was one of the main objectives of Gordon Brown's tax initiatives.[145] Having already cut the main rate of corporate income tax from 33 to 31 percent in the July 1997 budget, the Blair government made further cuts down to 30 percent beginning in FY 1999.[146] The rate for small firms was lowered from 21 to 20 percent, lower than in any other large industrial country.[147] *The Economist* lauded Britain's relatively low tax rates because they gave the country a competitive advantage.[148] The Advanced Corporation Tax, which required firms to prepay corporation taxes on dividends to shareholders, was abolished.[149] Over the long term, firms were expected to gain about £1.6 billion a year from these corporate tax changes, and the Treasury itself was expected to gain by £1 billion in 1999–2000 and £1.2 billion in 2000–1.[150]

Consistent with Clinton's strategy, the Blair government also sought dramatic reforms in the capital gains tax charged to individuals.[151] The reforms sought by the Blair government were designed specifically in accordance with some combination of monetarist-conservative directives shared by the Clinton administration for promoting long-term stability.[152] The reforms were meant to encourage greater investment in long-term rather than in short-term holdings.[153] The government further sought to give tax relief to serial entrepreneurs and small-time entrepreneurs by expanding the enterprise investment scheme.[154] In addition, taxes levied on gains made from selling shares or other assets would no longer be adjusted for inflation. At the time, the government stated that "assuming inflation sticks close to its target of 2.5 percent a year, those holding assets for only a couple years will pay more capital gains tax than now, and those holding for them for around 10 years will pay less."[155]

Clear similarities that existed in the tax policy strategies pursued by the Clinton and Blair administrations reflect their mutual commitment to similar core and secondary policy beliefs. Although all four administrations examined in this book share broad normative core beliefs, such as the proper scope of government and the belief in the merits of the market mechanism, Clinton and Blair pursued fiscal strategies that were more akin to those pursued by Thatcher and less so by Reagan. These contending beliefs shaped the political struggle that occurred over the adoption of both Gramm–Rudman in the United States and the medium-term financial strategy in Britain in the 1980s. In the 1980s in the United States, it appeared as though tax cutters would emerge as the dominant coalition on the final demise of the KWS. However, in the 1990s the outlook changed. As both the United States and Britain entered the new millennium with left-of-center governments at the helm, deficit reduction became the prevailing fiscal policy concern. Nevertheless, tax reform continued to represent an important, albeit secondary, issue of the neoliberal reform agenda in both countries.

Conclusion

Despite having experienced substantial setbacks in attaining their initial budgetary targets, Reagan's and Thatcher's deficit reduction efforts should by no means be regarded as a total loss. From a long-range view of policy change, it is clear that their governments were quite successful in fundamentally altering the scope of the policy discourse to include neoliberal ideas on the need for fiscal discipline and limited government. Although the Reagan and Thatcher administrations possessed different core and secondary fiscal beliefs, they both viewed big government and excessive public spending to be among the leading causes contributing to poor economic growth. Whatever their differences in core and secondary policy beliefs, the two governmental leaders and their supporters shared broadly similar core normative beliefs that were based the ideas of Hayek, Smith, and leading advocates belonging to the school of classic liberal economic thought.[156]

Despite possessing a strong intellectual commitment to neoliberalism, both the Reagan and the Thatcher governments failed to institute a permanent remedy to the deficit problem in their countries. Counter-intuitively, Clinton and Blair were successful in reframing several conservative policy issues in a manner that became palatable to the center-left in the United States and Britain. These two governments built a new type of coalition that incorporated many individuals from the traditional left (i.e., members of organized labor) as well as the traditional right (i.e., business groups). Both governments professed pursuing a third-way approach to political economy that relied on a unique mix of strategies from the left and right of center. This included welfare-to-work policies combined with free trade; increases in the minimum wage combined with tax cuts for small business; and earned income tax credits combined with cuts in welfare spending.

Timing was also a key factor that helped the deficit reduction cause in the Clinton–Blair era. This is due to the fact that emerging ideas and policies that stem from them often meet with formidable opposition from embedded status quo interest and other contending coalitions. Sufficient time must elapse for ideas to gain acceptance within the politics and policy mainstream. New ideas and strategies need to be tested over the course of at least one policy cycle before broad support can be reached on their effectiveness.[157] It was, therefore, easier for policy makers and the public alike to accept cuts in the growth of spending in the mid-1990s than it was in the early 1980s. The Clinton and Blair governments were instrumental in mobilizing and organizing additional members (new Democrats and modernizers) into the deficit reduction coalitions in both the United States and Britain. A wholesale commitment to eliminating the deficit was the logical extension of a core belief underlying the traditional deficit-reduction coalitions and their basic causal assumptions regarding prudent fiscal policy and economic growth. Over time, however, this stance became even more prominent in the policy agendas of both left-of-center parties.

Evaluating policy outcomes over a decade or more is necessary for gaining a comprehensive understanding of the effects of a policy on the subsystem and will enable policy actors to gain a reasonably accurate portrait of policy success and failure. According to Sabatier, "[N]umerous studies have shown that ambitious programs that appeared after a few years to be abject failures received more favorable evaluations when seen in a longer time frame; conversely initial success may evaporate over time."[158] If one were to evaluate the deficit-reduction initiatives undertaken by the Reagan and Thatcher administrations in the short term, those initiatives would most likely be regarded as disappointments. However, if they are evaluated over time, we gain an improved picture of how Reagan's and Thatcher's pioneering efforts in the 1980s provided the foundation for the shift that culminated in the late 1990s. Partisan convergence over the matter of spending restraint and deficit reduction provides strong evidence that a wholesale (neoliberal) paradigm shift has occurred in the US and British fiscal policy subsystems.

5 Summary

It has been just over a decade since Geoffrey Garrett and Peter Lange posed the question "What's Left for the Left?" in their seminal article dealing with left-of-center partisan governments in the modern era.[1] This book examines the role of ideas in helping us better understand partisan convergence in fiscal goals and strategies in the United States and Britain under Reagan Thatcher, Clinton, and Blair. Neoliberalism became the dominant paradigm in the fiscal policy discourse in both countries and has been embraced by moderates in the Republican and Democratic parties in the United States along with centrists in the Tory and Labour parties in Britain. In studying the influence of ideas on major shifts in fiscal policy over nearly two decades, we are able to provide a convincing account of a much more important, but elusive, phenomenon: the new left's success in enacting strategies that were initially espoused by the new right more than a decade earlier.

Although they are a critical part of budgetary policy making in the United States and Britain, interests and politics must be considered along with the role of ideas and causal beliefs. Interests are realized through causal understandings of policy problems and solutions. Causal beliefs about how the world works shape the way in which actors construe their interests. This, in turn, directly shapes their goals and the range of possible strategies that they may pursue. Purely rational-choice explanations of what drives political decisions assume that individuals know what is in their "interest" and make choices that will maximize their "expected utility." Despite their strengths, purely rational-choice explanations fail to account adequately for the many instances in which individuals who may be faced with similar constraints and opportunities nonetheless make very different choices. Rational behavior is itself derived through a system of causal beliefs that individuals hold about themselves and the social, political, and economic environments in which they live, work, trade, and vote. Because ideas and causal beliefs shape people's understanding of the world in which they live, these factors directly affect the range of desirable or "rational" choices that they may consider. Therefore, the way in which ideas are communicated among people is crucial to understanding major shifts in public policy over time. In the political arena, policy makers and other subsystem actors who share a similar set of core policy beliefs come together to advance a common policy agenda.

Ideas presented through policy paradigms or belief systems shape the policy debate within a subsystem. Policy paradigms embody core and secondary beliefs about the political environment and how that environment should be structured. Elite policy actors use policy paradigms to interpret the policy environment and their position within it. The concept of policy paradigms is based on Kuhn's model of scientific revolutions. Shifts in policy paradigms are driven by the accumulation of anomalies and the replacement of one paradigm by another set of ideas.

Major shifts in policy are examined within the context of political struggles between competing coalitions of policy actors within a policy subsystem.[2] Subsystem coalitions are organized around a set of common core elements of a belief system or paradigm that remain relatively stable for extended periods of time—usually a decade or more. These core elements are the basic causal assumptions that are widely shared by members of a coalition in a policy subsystem. Coalition actors are continuously learning and making empirical evaluations about the effects of their political strategies to realize their goals over time. They will likely continue strategies that they perceive will advance their core beliefs and substitute new strategies for those that they believe do not. Learning (through experience and feedback) is particularly important in developing and sustaining secondary aspects of policy beliefs. Because individuals in a coalition are highly unlikely to abandon core beliefs and will only do so under extraordinary conditions, most policy-oriented learning is normally confined to secondary aspects of a policy belief system.

Summary of the main arguments of the book

A neoliberal paradigm shift in the fiscal policy subsystem has occurred in the United States and Britain since the 1980s

Policy change and continuity over two decades was examined through a comparative analysis of the Reagan and Thatcher governments versus the Clinton and Blair governments. The evidence examined reveals that partisan convergence in economic ideas occurred beginning in the 1980s and was completed at the end of the 1990s. The shift entailed a fundamental change in the economic policy priorities of center-Left governments in the US and Britain from one focused on promoting full employment to one focused on promoting monetary stability. This economic strategy was consistent with a monetarist framework.

The ability of presidential or prime ministerial leaders to implement major economic policy change is dependent on their capacity to build broad support within a subsystem. This process involves what William Riker refers to as the art of *heresthetics*. Heresthetics is the framing of issues by political leaders in a manner that strategically seeks to weaken rival coalitions so as to advance one's own new winning coalition. Executive leaders, and the policy subsystems of which they are a part, are successful when they are able to neutralize the opposition and build a new political consensus around the coalition's core goals and beliefs.[3] The success of leaders and coalitions is dependent on material resources, such as compelling scientific evidence that supports a given coalition's claims on a policy issue, financial backing, votes, broad subsystem support, legal authority, and the like. The distribution of these material resources is often determined by factors that develop outside the policy subsystem but exert pressure for change within it. Over time, the cumulative effect of these pressures can culminate in a full-blown crisis, which can have the effect of promoting the position of minority coalitions in the policy discourse. Dimensions of a policy discourse are altered when new or contending views are added or old views are amended.

These external pressures may appear at first as anomalies perhaps in the form of a scientific breakthrough or unanticipated cataclysmic event that changes current understandings about the way in which the economy functions and operates. Over time, external shocks (whether they come in the form of emerging scientific evidence that seems to explain observed phenomena better or as a series of negative economic experiences that challenge the usefulness of existing policy remedies) may result in a full-blown crisis that can cause a major paradigm shift in a policy subsystem.[4] Neo-Keynesians in the United States and Britain held a core belief in the Phillips curve and the causal assumption that there was a necessary tradeoff between inflation and unemployment.[5] During the 1970s, "demand-managed" solutions continuously failed to alleviate persistent economic anomalies, such as stagflation. When the twin evils of inflation and unemployment reared themselves in the 1970s, neoliberal ideas began their gradual assent in the policy discourse. As economic conditions worsened in the late 1970s and into the early 1980s, more and more policy makers became convinced that existing public spending practices not only failed to remedy slow growth but in fact were a contributory cause of economic stagnation and unemployment.[6] During this time, a growing number of economic policy experts outside of the government (economists, policy makers, economic analysts) and other concerned groups (stockholders, concerned citizens, issue-oriented voters) also grew convinced that traditional government-driven remedies were inadequate for solving macroeconomic dilemmas.

As brought out in Chapter 2, crises themselves are often not apparent until coalitions, executives, or other leaders bring awareness to them. Participants need to have some means of evaluating a crisis to mobilize the necessary political and economic resources for grappling with eminent problems that are associated with it. A crisis must first be "diagnosed" before reigning beliefs can be challenged and new ones are introduced.[7] Neo-liberalism offered government officials and critical economic groups in the community an alternative view of the way in which the world works with respect to economic policy. Intellectual think tanks built with political leaders critical alliances that were heavily funded by some of the largest corporations in both countries. Their cause focused on limiting the sphere of government in the affairs of the private economy by launching a targeted assault on the two main mechanisms on which "big government" and the KWS (Keynesian welfare state) relied: progressive taxation and growing public expenditure for government programs. Neoliberals in both countries asserted that these twin redistributive engines were the main culprits in prohibiting new and much-needed private investment for immediate economic recovery and sustained long-term economic growth. Neoliberals asserted that the existing tax systems consistently failed to provide the correct incentives for promoting private investment. Similarly, they asserted that the spending proclivity that was directed toward growing welfare state programs led to excess borrowing in capital markets. By the 1980s, policy elites belonging to both the left and right of center in the United States and Britain grew concerned that large amounts of public borrowing were "crowding out" potential capital available to private investors.

Some of the most influential conservative thinkers and business executives came together to create a new intellectual infrastructure of neoliberal policy institutes. Leading the way were such conservatives as Irving Kristiol in the United States and William Rees-Mogg in Britain. By the mid-1980s, the American Enterprise, Heritage, Cato, and Hoover institutes had become critical players in initiating the neoliberal paradigm shift in the United States. The American Enterprise Institute's staff and board members were part of the nation's prominent business and political leadership.[8] *Thatcherites* played a pivotal role in the neoliberal intellectual establishment in Britain, by establishing the Centre for Policy Studies and building intellectual alliances with the Adam Smith Institute and so on.

By the mid-1980s, neoliberal Democrats established the Democratic Leadership Council (DLC) and the Progressive Policy Institute. The DLC made fiscal stability its overarching policy goal. By the early 1990s, Clinton, Gore, Tsongas, Nunn, and Gephardt took hold of the Democratic Party and made deficit reduction and investment-oriented tax relief the heart of the party's fiscal agenda. Following the lead of the new Democrats, such modernizers as Tony Blair, John Smith, Neil Kinnock, Gordon Brown, and the like in Britain's New Labour Party were also committed to the cause of fiscal discipline and promoting the growth of private capital through targeted investment tax reforms. Tony Blair's government built an ideational alliance with such influential figures as Anthony Giddens of the London School of Economics and with Geoff Mulgan of the Demos Policy Institute, which provided the intellectual support for the government's policy focus aimed at deepening human capital.

*Partisan convergence in the United States and Britain is both
strongly indicative of, and intrinsically related to, a broad shift in
the reigning paradigm governing a policy subsystem*

A study that focuses on ideas in explaining major shifts in policy goals and
outcomes may illuminate several critical points about partisan convergence
that may have been inadequately addressed in other studies. Policy makers
and the voters alike in the United States and Britain now view fiscal policy
and the role of government in the economy in terms fundamentally different
from those of only a generation ago. This development will have several
implications for the future of economic policy in the United States and Britain.
We have already witnessed dramatic welfare reform in the United States,
and interviews that were conducted in the Blair government suggest that
Britain is headed on a similar course. For example, the Clinton and Blair
administrations imposed strict time limits on benefit claimants, and both
governments pursued fiscal policy goals in accordance with monetary
imperatives.

It is not an easy task to demonstrate the causal influence of ideas in shaping
the policy choices of executive leaders. It is even more difficult to show
conclusively that a certain set of ideas may have been responsible for shaping
a specific policy shift. This is especially true in the case of the United States,
where the structure of the economic policy system is relatively fragmented,
given its separation of powers. Complicating matters further, political fragmentation extends within the executive branch itself. This is mainly due to
the considerable change in staff and personnel in the highest levels of the
bureaucracy that invariably accompanies every new presidential administration.[9] Despite this, we can observe remarkable consistency in fiscal policy
from one partisan government to the next. Take, for instance, the broad
continuity of Keynes-guided fiscal policy that occurred over the course of
four successive administrations beaaring various partisan colors: Johnson
(D), Nixon (R), Ford (R), and even Carter (D). All four regimes followed
fiscal trends that were supported by the KWS (with some modifications) in
the design of fiscal policy. Despite America's relatively fragmented political
structure, certain ideas, it seems, have the ability to transcend partisan and
even institutional divisions. Given this, we are faced with a compelling
question: under what conditions does this phenomenon occur? What role, if
any, does a shift in partisan governance play in that process? Partisanship is
only half the story.

Politically ambitious leaders belonging to minority parties or coalitions
(or both) may adopt the ideas and rhetoric of majority parties or coalitions
in accordance with their own policy slant and political reasoning. The
explanation behind policy paradigm shifts goes well beyond a simple change
in partisan rule. Partisanship is, of course, an important dynamic incorporated
in our explanation of major policy shifts and, therefore, analyzed here within
the context of policy subsystems. Also, it must be noted that new policy

concerns and issues are often introduced into the discourse by members who share both a common partisan persuasion and ideological disposition. The fact that governments of different partisan persuasions pursued distinct policy strategies within a broadly similar neoliberal framework of ideas is compelling and provides strong evidence that ideas are more than just political flak. Despite their varied strategies and partisan affiliations, Reagan, Thatcher, Clinton, and Blair all adhered to a rather well-defined set of neoliberal principles and policy guidelines that called for limiting overall government interference in the private sphere and deferring to market mechanisms whenever possible for allocating societal resources. These general principles influenced all four governments and their mutual pursuit to limit government expenditure, to reduce taxes, and to deregulate (or privatize) services whenever possible.

The shift from the KWS paradigm to neoliberlism was motivated by a combination of economic expertise, electoral politics, and economic anomalies. It was the product of an enduring process that was initiated by a grass-roots political movement that ran counter to the ideological premise of the KWS and supporters of big government in the United States.[10] Neoliberals built an intellectual base for policy change by establishing research institutes and think tanks, such as the American Enterprise Institute, the Cato Institute, the Heritage Foundation, and the like. Neoliberalism also generated appeal among key members of the elite media and such news organizations as the *Wall Street Journal* and *The Economist* (among others) and among powerful business lobby groups. Neoliberalism was further vindicated in the policy discourse by the Clinton administration and the DLC along with the Progressive Policy Institute. These "new Democrats" shared the belief in self-sufficiency and individual rather than collective initiative as the source of economic growth. These beliefs represented a fundamental departure from the redistributive logic behind the KWS.

There has been broad ideational continuity in the fiscal policy goals and strategies of the right- and left-of-center governments in Britain since 1979 as well. Ideas are the central factor in explaining the policy shift. Neoliberalism was supported by an intellectual infrastructure that includes leading researchers at such think tanks as the Adam Smith Institute, the Institute of Directors, the Centre for Policy Studies and the Institute of Economic Affairs.[11] These think tanks were part of a policy subsystem that further included such business groups as the Confederation of British Industry, important elite journalists in major publications (e.g., *Financial Times*), and numerous independent economists.[12]

Prime Minister Blair appointed neoliberal economists and policy makers within the internal advisory system of the Treasury and other ministries, such as Social Security, the Department for Education and Employment, and others. Interviews with key advisers serving under the Prime Minister, the Chancellor of the Exchequer, the Chief Secretary to the Treasury, and the other important economic ministers (including the Paymaster-General, the

Financial Secretary to the Treasury, the Economic Secretary to the Treasury, etc.) confirm this. Whitehall's current leaders have made fiscal prudence and transparency the central tenets of economic policy. Blair and the modernizers proceeded according to the belief that governments must dedicate themselves to the cause of promoting economic growth through greater private investment in Britain's economy. *Blairites* have sought to reduce the country's overall public debt to ensure a sound economic system that could woo new private investment. Under Blair's leadership, the Treasury formally introduced specific limits on government spending and borrowing. The most compelling neoliberal change, however, has been the Blair government's decision to grant the Bank of England monetary autonomy for setting short-term interest rates. In taking these actions, the Labour Party has fundamentally altered its traditional relationship toward business interests and the private sector.

Differences in the neoliberal fiscal policy strategies pursued by the Reagan and Thatcher administrations reflect differences in their core and secondary policy beliefs

Chapter 3 argues that differences between the strategies pursued by Reagan and Thatcher reflect their differing core and secondary policy beliefs. Core aspects of a belief system represent the most important concerns of executive leaders, and the coalitions of which they are a part. At the same time, secondary aspects of a belief system are also important, albeit to a lesser degree than that of core aspects. Reagan's core commitment to the Laffer-curve supply-side approach and the belief that redistributive progressive taxation was most directly responsible for poor economic performance encouraged him to pursue tax reduction as the core issue and deficit reduction as an important, but secondary, issue. We then compared these beliefs with those of Thatcher, who proceeded according to the logic that fiscal imprudence was most responsible for poor economic performance. Following this basic logic, Thatcher pursued deficit reduction as the core policy issue and tax reform as an important, but secondary, issue. The overriding policy priority governing Reagan's initial fiscal agenda was to liberate private wealth to spur entrepreneurial activity by reducing taxes on individual income. By way of contrast, the Thatcher strategy focused first and foremost on liberating capital from the hands of government for private investors by reducing Britain's deficit. Their discrete strategies represent distinct manifestations of the neoliberal paradigm shift.

Both Reagan's and Thatcher's failure to attain balanced budgets is an important theme of this book. It is often asserted that Reagan's inability to balance the budget was due mostly to the fact that he was constrained by the separation of powers wherein the Democrat-controlled Congress blocked the initiatives of the Republican administration in its attempts to control fiscal expenditure. Although partly true, this explanation fails to account for the fact that Thatcher, who presided over a unitary system, nonetheless experienced comparable setbacks and disappointments. The Thatcher government should have been well positioned for instituting the large spending cuts deemed necessary for eliminating the budget deficit. Reagan and Thatcher actually encountered the same problem: the politics of blame avoidance.[13] Although the Reagan administration was constrained by the separation of powers, the Thatcher government was constrained by what Paul Pierson calls the "concentration of accountability."[14] Therefore, these institutional differences cancel each other.

In evaluating why deficit spending has generated so much concern in the economic policy discourse in recent times, one cannot ignore the pivotal role of policy learning. Policy makers have adjusted their positions in light of a growing body of empirical evidence regarding the national deficit and its effect on real and potential investment. According to Michael Boskin, by the mid-1980s, policy makers in the United States began heeding empirical findings "that deficits contribute to high interest rates, both directly through government borrowing in credit markets, and indirectly through uncertainty over their likely economic effects."[15]

Although it could not break the pattern in which federal spending continued to increase as a percentage of GNP, the Reagan administration was able to slow the rate of increase of government outlays from "an inflation-adjusted real growth rate of about 44 percent to 33 percent in Reagan's first term in office, then to about 18 percent during his second term."[16] In bringing about these modest cuts in the rate of increase in government expenditure, the Reagan administration sought to undermine one of the critical support beams of the KWS. These ideas laid the foundation for the deficit reduction agenda that would be championed by the Clinton administration almost a decade later.[17]

In Britain, the Thatcher–Howe leadership believed (along with their core supporters in the Treasury) that fiscal stability could be obtained only through substantial cuts in the public sector borrowing requirement (the national deficit).[18] The medium-term financial strategy stated in very precise terms that tax increases (in certain areas) would be necessary to pay for existing public programs.[19] The strategy focused on reducing the rate of price inflation through a steady reduction in the rate of monetary growth and through meaningful cuts in both spending and borrowing. The medium-term financial strategy shifted the emphasis from fiscal to monetary policy.

Both the Reagan and Thatcher administrations were unable to secure from key subsystem actors the required support that would have been necessary to subvert or neutralize the efforts of politicians, administrative agencies, and economists who supported existing spending trends in social policy. Deficit spending had become inextricably linked with expensive social policies and programs that were considered by many (belonging to both the left and right of center) to be sacred cows. Although there was broad support for the general cause of reducing government waste and unchecked spending, many

Laffer-curve supply-siders in the United States and populists and Tory wets and damps in Britain were not prepared to make the austere cuts in popular social programs. Tax cutters in the Republican Party in the United States and populists, wets, and damps within the Tory party in Britain thus actually ended up supporting policies that led to increases in public spending.

Both Reagan and Thatcher often found that they could not even count on the necessary support from members within their own cabinets, let alone broad support among the general membership within their own parties.[20] Balancing the budget in the United States and Britain entailed a major shift in political and economic priorities. In the final analysis, both governments failed to cultivate broad support within the fiscal policy subsystem for the kinds of spending cuts that would have been necessary to eliminate the deficit within their own countries. When one takes into consideration the political constraints that Reagan and Thatcher faced in their attempts to eliminate their deficits, the budgetary disappointments they experienced are not surprising. Both Reagan and Thatcher attempted to reverse public spending trends that had become embedded in their countries' political systems over nearly half a century. At the same time, however, both leaders were aware of the fact that they could not reduce the deficit without curbing existing trends in public spending through some cuts in politically popular programs.[21]

From the time they took power, Reagan and Thatcher faced a common constraint: the recession of the early 1980s. Early success or failure in implementing their policy agendas would set strong precedents that would follow the Reagan and Thatcher administrations throughout their tenures in office. Both leaders, therefore, were under tremendous pressure to secure undisputed gains early in their administrations to bolster their credibility on the deficit issue. In light of this fact, the recession could not have come at a worse time for the two conservative leaders. The recession created additional gaps between receipts and outlays that would have to be filled through cuts in public spending even deeper than those originally projected. Many politicians in the United States and Britain ultimately found the notion of cutting popular social programs in the midst of an economic recession to be too risky politically. Initially, Thatcher sought to raise taxes and tighten fiscal policy in an effort to cut the money supply but found it nearly impossible to do so in the midst of a depression.[22] In the final analysis, the issue of spending cuts led in her 1981 cabinet to a major political struggle that Thatcher and her supporters in the Treasury lost.[23]

Owing to the ambitious nature of his tax cut agenda, Reagan treated the deficit issue with a certain benign neglect.[24] In fact, most of the spending cuts that would have been required to balance the budget were not explicitly identified in Reagan's budget proposals.[25] By the time the economic recovery began in the mid-1980s, Reagan had already lost his credibility on the deficit issue in Congress. More generally, the political momentum that was behind his early budget successes with Congress had waned.

Reducing the tax burden on wealthy individuals in theory represented an area wherein Thatcher's and Reagan's policies were highly consistent with one another. Thatcher was able to cultivate support within various Tory Party groups (populists, wets, and drys) to enact a series of important reforms that fundamentally altered the tax structure in Britain. Over the course of her 12-year reign, Thatcher delivered substantial cuts in the marginal income tax rate, reduced top and bottom rates for the country's rich, introduced significant cuts in capital gains taxes, and abolished both the investment income surcharge and social security (National Insurance).[26] At the same time, however, Thatcher enacted the highly contentious poll tax on local authorities and imposed new taxes on North Sea oil profits to pay for tax cuts to employers and investors.

Counter-intuitively, both Thatcher's and Reagan's tax policies ultimately resulted in tax increases on corporate income. This is particularly evident in the case of the United States, where cuts in individual income taxes were ultimately paid for by imposing greater tax burdens on corporate income. In signing the final tax bill that caused the shifting of the tax burden onto corporate profits, Reagan compromised secondary aspects of his policy agenda to preserve a core aspect: alleviating the tax burden on personal income.

Striking similarities in the fiscal policy strategies pursued by the Clinton and Blair administrations reflect these leaders' mutual commitment to similar core policy beliefs

Labour Party modernizers were intellectually aligned with the neoliberal policy views of new Democrats. Top-level officials and advisors in the British Treasury frequently met with their US counterparts and other senior economists in the US Democratic administration to discuss how new Labour should proceed in carrying out economic reform. Gordon Brown and Lawrence Summers, for example, shared the belief that economic growth was dependent on increasing the amount of private capital available for private investment. Modernizers in the Labour party were inspired by the DLC initiative in moving the US Democratic Party to the center so as to capture the support of new constituencies. Modeling Clinton and the new Democrats, Blair and the modernizers sought to build electoral support among Britain's business community (known as the *City*) and the middle class.[27]

Policy makers grew increasingly concerned about the effects of deficit spending on long-term interest rates and declining levels of private investment. These developments, coupled with the effects of economic transformation from manufacturing-based economies to the service-based, caused policy makers on both sides of the partisan divide to reexamine their policy beliefs. Here, the issue of timing was a critical factor. A growing consensus composed of moderates and conservatives belonging to both parties began to view the deficit as a vital economic issue that threatened the growth of financial investment.[28]

***The ability of Clinton and Blair to consolidate and complete the
neoliberal fiscal paradigm shift that was initiated by Reagan and
Thatcher was rooted in heresthetics***

The success of Clinton and Blair in the area of deficit reduction rests in their
ability to reframe several conservative policy issues in a manner that allowed
them to build a new coalition incorporating many individuals from the
traditional left (e.g., members of organized labor) as well as the traditional
right (e.g., business groups) by pursuing a third-way-inspired strategy. This
strategy was based on a unique mix of policies that included instituting
welfare-to-work policies while expanding small business tax cuts and
increasing the minimum wage while cutting welfare expenditure.

Successful completion of a major shift in policy requires at least a decade
or more to provide sufficient time for policy to undergo at least one full
cycle of formulation, implementation, evaluation, and reformulation. Over
the course of time, KWS ideas and strategies continued to be implemented
and reviewed for their effectiveness. This process enabled policy makers to
gain a deeper empirical understanding of the effects of deficit spending on
the overall health of the economy. Specifically, members belonging to both
the left and right of center in both countries witnessed the effects of deficit
spending in creating high long-term interest rates and subsequent declines in
the levels of productive investment.

These conditions created a hospitable environment for the testing of
neoliberal strategies and policies that focused on spending reductions for
social programs, experiments with tax reform, and so on. By the 1990s,
deficit reduction and targeted tax cuts for investment had become the rallying
cry for new Democrats and New Labour. The US economic expansion of the
1990s represented the final death-blow to the KWS and traditional beliefs
that increased spending would be needed to produce an economic recovery.
In the midst of this expansion, political support for the deficit reduction
cause expanded.

Although neoliberal ideas had been gaining support in the Labour Party
since the 1980s, the Blair government's commitment to fiscal stability was
heavily reinforced by the enormous US economic recovery that occurred
during the Clinton era. In addition, prolonged economic recessions in France
and Germany during the same period were blamed on their *dirigiste* or
government-led interventionist-style policy strategies that were based on their
so-called Rhenish model of political economy. These factors encouraged the
Blair government in its belief in neoliberalism as the best approach for solving
Britain's economic problems. Policy makers in the Treasury became convinced
that the neoliberal path that they followed provided them with a set of
superior policy tools for dealing with economic adjustment as compared to
their European counterparts, who were relying more heavily on government-
led fiscal policies for economic recovery.

The United States and Britain: a glimpse of the road ahead

At the time of writing (2003), a number of noteworthy developments have occurred in the US and British fiscal agenda. Unlike his predecessors of the last 20 years, George W. Bush does not seem to embrace a coherent framework of economic ideas. This is evidenced by the very narrowly focused fiscal policies that have been aimed exclusively on cutting marginal tax rates for America's wealthiest individual income earners while showing virtually no tendencies for fiscal restraint in discretionary spending (which has been growing at nearly eight percent a year). Back in the year 2000, the federal government estimated that the United States would accrue budget surpluses totaling approximately $5.6 trillion over the next decade.[29] With that kind of excess revenue coming into the Treasury, it was not unreasonable for George W. Bush to want to give a portion of the tax revenues back to those who were "overcharged" in the 1990s. Over the next three years, however, the government witnessed massive reductions in those revenues. The reduction in government receipts was related to a number of developments over which the Bush administration initially had little direct control. The market dropped by $2 trillion in the summer of 2002, which led to major declines in capital gains tax receipts and taxes paid on cashing in stock options.[30] When George W. Bush came to power in 2001, the Dow Jones Industrial Average was at 10,600 points but later dipped below 8,000, echoing the 24 percent drop of the Wall Street crash of 1929.[31] In April of 2002, individual income tax receipts declined by 36 percent.[32] That translates into a $150 billion reduction from the previous year.[33] Also, there is credible evidence that about one-third of the revenue shortage could be structural in nature and that receipts would probably be $400 billion to $600 billion lower than originally calculated over the next decade. In the 1990s, such legislation as the Budget Enforcement Act imposed fixed ceilings on discretionary spending and mandated that any new tax cuts or spending increases be revenue-neutral. This meant that any new tax cuts had to be offset by tax increases imposed somewhere else and that any increases in entitlement spending would have to be offset by cuts in discretionary spending. When the budget was balanced in the late 1990s, the concern over spending growth began to diminish somewhat. The tax and spending proposals favored by the George W. Bush administration have not been focused on fiscal stability. Bush lobbied hard to get $75 billion for military action in Iraq, and the president signed a costly farm bill that is expected to add $170 billion in new spending over the next decade.[34] Deficit spending for FY 2003–4 is expected to reach as high as $160 billion (1.5 percent of GDP).[35] If George W. Bush's tax cuts are made permanent and spending continues to rise at its current rate, the deficit will reach as high as $5.4 trillion over the next decade (not computing the current entitlement surplus).[36] As increasing numbers of baby boomers retire and start drawing on their Social Security and Medicare, there will be substantial increases in entitlement spending that will drain the entitlement surplus relatively quickly.[37]

The fiscal course followed by George W. Bush is not terribly surprising, given the fact that economic issues, save his tax cut plan, played almost no role in his election campaign against Al Gore. Unlike the situations in 1980 and 1992, during the 2000 election the US economy was still going strong. Therefore, economic stability and productivity growth did not play as important a role in the campaign rhetoric of the 2000 election as they had in prior elections. In the election of 2000, voters seemed to be focused more on the personalities of the two candidates, rather than on the substance of their fiscal policies. Bush's policy indifference toward fiscal stability and its impact on long-term capital investment is evidenced by a number of factors. The Bush administration came into power without ever establishing an effective economic policy leadership.[38] Such leadership is regarded as critical for providing information and, when necessary, assurance to investors about the state of the economy and the White House's commitment to economic stability. As Bush's first Treasury Secretary, Paul O'Neil would have been the person best suited for this position. O'Neil's failure to provide sufficient leadership in inspiring investor confidence has frustrated traditional conservatives and monetarists. High investor confidence in Clinton's economic policies was directly related to the competence of his economic team. Clinton's Treasury Secretaries (Robert Rubin and later Lawrence Summers) were well respected among Wall Street investors because of their "unyielding commitment to market-friendly standards and principles during economic instability that occurred in the fall of 1997 and in the late 1990s."[39] Having no clear leadership in place, the Bush administration appeared rudderless and disoriented when the economy slowed and market instability arose.

Deficit cutters and other traditional conservatives began lobbying the Bush administration to take decisive measures to address the fears of investors. Bush responded to the pressure by replacing senior members of his economic team of tax cutters with a group of deficit cutters. Treasury Secretary Paul O'Neill was replaced by John Snow, former head of the railroad giant CSX; NEC Chairman Larry Lindsey was replaced by Stephen Friedman of Goldman Sachs; and SEC Chairman Harvey Pitt was replaced by William Donaldson.[40] Although traditional conservative deficit cutters lauded the change, the new team was not as warmly received by tax cutters. Tax cutters both inside and outside government raised strong objections to the new team of deficit cutters. Most outspoken among them was Stephen Moore, who heads the antitax political action committee called the *Club for Growth*.[41] Moore and his tax-cutter colleagues strongly objected to the appointment of Stephen Friedman because of his heavy involvement with a bipartisan group of deficit cutters called the *Concord Coalition*, which he formerly led.[42] Moore and his "pro-growth" coalitional allies also objected to John Snow because of his leadership role with a pressure group of CEO deficit cutters called the *Business Round-table*, devoted to reducing the nation's deficit. Snow, in particular, was instrumental in facilitating during the Clinton era the historic deficit-reduction compromise that involved raising taxes.[43]

Democrat and Republican deficit cutters in the Senate, such as Senators Jon Corzine (D-NJ), Pete Domenici (R-NM), and Charles Grassley (R-IA, the incoming Senate Finance Committee chairman), are concerned that Bush's 2003–4 $300 billion tax cut proposal (meant to supplement the existing $1.35 trillion tax package he got last year) will result in large deficits that will endanger the very fragile economic recovery by driving up long-term interest rates as they did in the early 1990s.[44]

When the Blair government assumed power in 1997, the new Chancellor of the Exchequer, Gordon Brown, committed the Treasury to tight fiscal budgets. This strategy has served Britain well. The government was not only able to end years of structural deficit spending but actually produced a series of budget surpluses that lasted until this year. These fiscal conditions raised the esteem of the Blair government and its policies within the business community. The Blair government achieved an unprecedented electoral victory in 2002. Just prior to this, Brown confidently announced a significant increase in public expenditure over the next three years with the purpose of improving the public services.[45] Since that time, however, things have turned around dramatically. Instead of the promised budget surpluses, the fiscal pendulum has swung toward deficit spending once again. The Blair government borrowed £20 billion this last fiscal year and is expected to borrow £24 billion for FY 2003–4.[46]

The question is how this new borrowing will affect the fiscal stability that the Blair government has worked so hard to achieve. New spending and the return to budget deficits by the Blair government might lead critics to conclude that the Blair government has simply returned to the traditional spend-and-borrow policies of the old Labour Party. On the surface, cynics who challenge Blair's pure commitment to neoliberalism and fiscal stability seem to have a solid case. On deeper examination, however, the picture appears much more sophisticated. During the economic growth spurt that Britain experienced in the late 1990s, tax revenues were temporarily high, owing to high profits generated by the financial services industry and an increase in the number of wealthy tax payers.[47] During this period, the Treasury under the leadership of Brown kept spending to relatively low levels. Keeping spending tight during the growth period generated unprecedented surpluses. Now that the British economy has slowed and tax receipts have been sharply reduced, the Blair government can afford some "wiggle room" to increase spending and borrowing in the short term to increase demand temporarily without seriously jeopardizing stability.[48] According to *The Economist*, "[U]nlike beleaguered euro-area finance ministers who are subject to the rigid constraints of the stability pact, Mr Brown's fiscal rules take account of the state of the economic cycle, so that he can borrow more freely when the economy is weak. The government has the lowest ratio of debt to GDP among the G-7 club of rich industrialized countries."[49] Under the circumstances, Brown's borrowing policies do not appear to be fiscally disastrous, at least in the short term. The question is whether deficit spending will be extended and what the long-term consequences will be for the economy. Britain has been served well by the current government's commitment to fiscal prudence. What happens next, however, remains to be seen.

Notes

1 Policy ideas and partisan convergence

1 We adopt Theodore Lowi's definition of redistributive policy that he distinguishes from regulatory and distributive types of policies. Theodore Lowi, "American Business, Public Policy, Case Studies, and Political Theory," *World Politics*, 16 (1964), pp. 687–91. Lowi defines each policy type according to its impact or expected impact on society. Each policy type is functionally distinct and corresponds to real phenomena and establishes real arenas of power encompassing political structure, political process, elites, and group relationships. It is useful, therefore, to separate redistributive sorts of policies from the other two. Redistributive policies are highly distinctive in their nature and impact from that of regulatory and distributive types of policies. Their "categories of impact" are much broader in scope. The primary decisional locus for redistributive types of policy is the executive and peak associations. As distinguished from redistributive types of policy, distributive policies can be regarded as the ultimate form of "patronage" or "pork" and are identified by the ease with which they can be desegregated and allocated in relative isolation from other resources. They are best thought of as highly individualized decisions that, when taken collectively, comprise a policy. Classic examples include traditional tariffs, defense procurement, research and development, and the like. The primary decisional locus of distributive policies is the congressional committee or agency (or both). Regulatory policies, much like distributive policies, are specific and individual in their impact. Regulatory policies are not easily disaggregated and tend to accumulate among all individuals. The primary decisional locus of regulatory types of policy is found in the Congressional arena.
2 Nigel Boyle, *Crafting Change: Labor Market Policy Under Mrs Thatcher* (forthcoming), p. 6, Ch. 1.
3 Please see Peter Hall, "Policy Paradigms, Social Learning and the State: The Case of Economic Policy Making in Britain," *Comparative Politics*, (1993), pp. 275–96; Peter Hall, ed., *The Political Power of Economic Ideas: Keynesianism Across Nations* (Princeton, NJ: Princeton University Press, 1989).
4 Paul A. Sabatier, "Policy Change Over a Decade or More," in Paul A. Sabatier and Hank C. Jenkins-Smith, eds, *Policy Change and Learning: An Advocacy Coalition Approach* (Boulder, CO: Westview Press, 1993), pp. 16–17.
5 Ibid., p. 25.
6 Paul Sabatier and Neil Pelkey, "Incorporating Multiple Actors and Guidance Instruments into Models of Regulatory Policymaking: An Advocacy Coalition Framework," *Administration and Society*, 19 (1987), pp. 236–63, p. 237.
7 Paul A. Sabatier, "Policy Change Over a Decade or More," p. 26.
8 We draw heavily on insights presented by John F. Munro on similarities between the ACF and Thomas Kuhn's notion of scientific paradigms and apply them to our comparison of

Peter Hall's policy paradigm approach and the ACF. See John F. Munro, "California Water Politics: Explaining Policy Change in a Cognitively Polarized System," in Paul A. Sabatier and Hank C. Jenkins Smith, eds, *Policy Change and Learning* (Boulder, CO: Westview Press, 1993), pp. 105–27.

9 Paul A. Sabatier, "Policy Change Over a Decade or More," p. 33.

10 Definition of "neoliberalism" taken from *The McGraw-Hill Dictionary of Modern Economics* (New York: McGraw-Hill Inc., 1983), pp. 318–19.

11 Andrew Gamble, *Hayek: The Iron Cage of Liberty* (Boulder, CO: Westview Press, 1996), pp. 100–1.

12 Michael J. Boskin, *Reagan and the Economy: The Successes, Failures and Unfinished Agenda* (San Francisco: ICS Press, 1987), p. 1.

13 Edward Nell, *Free Market Conservatism: A Critique of Theory and Practice* (London: George Allen and Unwin, 1984), p. 11. Michael Boskin substantiates this claim for the Reagan administration in Michael Boskin, *Reagan and the Economy*, pp. 2–3.

14 William Niskanen, *Reaganomics: An Insider's Account of the People and Politics* (New York: Oxford University Press, 1988), p. 19.

15 J. Harold McClure and Thomas D. Willett, "Understanding the Supply-Siders," in Craig Stubblebine and Thomas D. Willett, eds, *Reaganomics: A Midterm Report* (San Francisco: ICS Press, 1983), p. 64.

16 Edward Nell, *Free Market Conservatism*, p. 11.

17 Harold D. Clarke, Marianne C. Stewart, and Gary Zuk, "Introduction: Three Political Economies in an Era of Economic Decline," in Clarke, Harold D., Stewart, Marianne C., and Zuk, Gary, eds, *Economic Decline and Political Change: Canada, Great Britain, and the United States* (Pittsburgh: University of Pittsburgh Press, 1989), p. 9.

18 Ibid.

19 Ibid.

20 Ibid.

21 Ibid.

22 Patrick Akard, "The Return of the Market?: Reflections of the Real Conservative Tradition in US Policy Discourse," *Sociological Inquiry*, 65, No. 3–4 (1995), pp. 286–308, p. 295.

23 Herbert Stein, *Presidential Economics: The Making of Economic Policy from Roosevelt to Clinton* (Washington, DC: American Enterprise Institute Press, 1994), p. 448.

24 William Riker, *The Art of Political Manipulation* (New York: Yale University Press, 1986).

25 Peter Hall, "Policy Paradigms, Social Learning and the State: The Case of Economic Policy Making in Britain," *Comparative Politics*, 25 (Apr 1993), pp. 275–96. Macroeconomic efforts to reduce unemployment were rejected in Britain in favor of balanced budgets and direct tax reductions, p. 284.

26 Paul A. Sabatier, *Policy Change Over a Decade or More*, p. 16.

27 Paul Pierson, "The Deficit and Politics of Domestic Reform," in Margaret Weir, ed., *The Social Divide: Political Parties and the Future of Activist Government* (Washington, DC: Brookings Institution Press, 1998), p. 137.

28 Frank R. Baumgartner and Bryan D. Jones, *Agendas and Instability in American Politics* (Chicago: University of Chicago Press, 1993), p. 39.

29 Ibid., p. 16.

30 In *Reaganomics*, (1988): 23, William Niskanen makes the point that Reagan had no mandate to make the massive cuts in domestic spending that he originally proposed. We have extended this basic point to argue that if leaders are to be successful in bringing about major changes in public policy, they must possess sufficient political support within a given subsystem to do so.

31 See William Riker, *The Art of Political Manipulation*, p. x.

32 Ibid., p. 18.

33 Bob Woodward, *The Agenda: Inside the Clinton White House* (New York: Simon & Schuster, 1994), p. 98.

34 Martin Walker, *The President We Deserve: Bill Clinton, His Rise, Falls, and Comebacks* (New York: Crown Publishers, 1996), p. 309.

35 The term *efficiency hypothesis* is cited from Geoffrey Garrett, "Capital Mobility, Trade, and Domestic Politics," in Robert O. Keohane and Helen V. Milner, *Internationalization and Domestic Politics* (Cambridge: Cambridge University Press, 1996), p. 90.

36 *See* David Andrews. "Capital Mobility and State Autonomy: Toward a Structural Theory of International Monetary Relations," *International Studies Quarterly*. 38, No. 2 (June 1994), pp. 193–218; John Goodman and Louis Pauly, "The Obsolescence of Capital Controls? Economic Management in an Age of Global Markets," *World Politics*, 46 (1993), pp. 50–82; Paulette Kurzer, *Business and Banking: Political Change and Economic Integration in Western Europe* (Ithaca: Cornell University Press, 1993); M. Webb, "International Economic Structures, Government Interests, and International Coordination of Macroeconomic Adjustment Policies," *International Organization*, 45 (1991), pp. 309–42. The central claim of the international capital mobility thesis is that when capital is eminently mobile across international borders, the sustainable macroeconomic policy options available to states are systematically circumscribed.

37 Geoffrey Garrett. "Capital Mobility, Trade, and the Domestic Politics of Economic Policy," in Robert O. Keohane and Helen V. Milner, eds, *Internationalization and Domestic Politics* (Cambridge: Cambridge University Press, 1996), p. 88.

38 For further studies on this theme, see David Andrews, "Capital Mobility and State Autonomy: Towards a Structural Theory of International Monetary Relations," *International Studies Quarterly*, 38, No. 2 (June 1994), pp. 193–218; Paulette Kurzer, *Business and Banking: Political Change and Economic Integration In Western Europe* (Ithaca: Cornell University Press, 1993); Ton Notermans, "The Abdication of National Policy Autonomy," *Politics and Society* 21 (June 1993), pp. 133–67; Fritz Scharpf, *Crisis and Choice in European Social Democracy* (Ithaca: Cornell University Press, 1991).

39 Mark Hallerberg and William Roberts Clark, "How Should Political Scientists Measure Capital Mobility? A Review," paper prepared for presentation at the 1997 Annual Meeting of the American Political Science Association, Washington, DC, August 28–31, p. 2.

40 Ibid.

41 Simon Lee, "The Political Economy of the Third Way," paper presented at the Global Turbulence: Crisis in National and International Political Economy Conference, Simon Fraser University, July 2001, p. 1.

42 In "The Political Economy of the Third Way," paper presented at the Global Turbulence Instability in National and International Political Economy Conference, Vancouver, Canada, 2001, p. 1, Simon Lee brings out that "in the first quarter of 2001 portfolio investment abroad from the UK was 34.9 billion pounds (compared to portfolio investment in the UK of £23.7 billion) while other investment abroad totaled £186.1 billion (compared to record investment of £200.3 billion in the UK)."

43 The Bank of England has since made the decision to reduce interest rates gradually (over a five-month period) but only after having achieved domestic fiscal stability. Chancellor's Budget Statement, *Financial Times*, March 1999.

44 Simon Lee, "The Political Economy of the Third Way," paper presented at the Global Turbulence: Crisis in National and International Political Economy Conference, Simon Fraser University, July 2001, p. 1.

45 *The Economist*, 9 June 2001, p. 10.

46 Ibid.

47 Ibid.

48 Robert Geyer asserts convincingly that even the pro-EU orientation of Blair's New Labour government was not a direct consequence of external economic pressures. Rather, he suggests that the left's pro-EU position developed out of domestic political concerns. Geyer argues that it was "Modernisers" or centrists in the Labour Party itself that used the pro-EU position as rhetorical strategy for gaining the political support necessary to bring about change in party structure and policy. Robert Geyer, "Globalization and the

(Non-) Defense of the Welfare State," *West European Politics*, 121, No. 3 (1998), pp. 77–102, p. 90.

49 See Eric Helleiner, *States and the Reemergence of Global Finance: From Bretton Woods to the 1990s* (Ithaca: Cornell University Press, 1994), and Louis Pauly, *Opening Financial Markets: Banking Politics on the Pacific Rim* (Ithaca: Cornell University Press, 1998).

50 Eric Helleiner in *States and the Reemergence of Global Finance,* cited in David Andrews and Thomas Willett, "Financial Interdependence and the State: International Monetary Relations at Century's End," *International Organization*, 51 (1997), pp. 479–511, p. 481.

51 In David Andrews and Thomas Willett, "Financial Interdependence and the State," *International Organization*, 51 (1997), pp. 479–511, p. 491. Andrews and Willett give considerable credit to the "international transmission of changed ideas about inflation as an explanatory variable that drove the disinflationary convergence of the industrial countries as opposed to the international transmission of direct economic effects."

52 The Downsian explanation of convergence posits that major parties will assume similar policy stances once a winning program is discovered, so as to gain the maximum amount of votes possible. For a more complete explanation, see Anthony Downs, *An Economic Theory of Democracy* (New York: Harper and Row, 1957).

53 Judith Goldstein and Robert O. Keohane, "Ideas and Foreign Policy: An Analytic Framework," in Judith Goldstein and Robert O. Keohane, eds, *Ideas and Foreign Policy: Beliefs, Institutions, and Political Change* (Ithaca: Cornell University Press, 1993), p. 4.

54 Ibid., p. 6.

55 A.T. Denzau and Douglass C. North, "Shared Mental Models: Ideologies and Institutions," *Kyklos*, 47 (1994), pp. 3–31.

56 Judith Goldstein and Robert O. Keohane. "Ideas and Foreign Policy," p. 3.

57 Ibid., p. 13.

58 See Arthur T. Denzau and Douglass C. North, "Shared Mental Models," pp. 3–31.

59 Ibid., p. 18.

60 Judith Goldstein and Robert O. Keohane, "Ideas and Foreign Policy," p. 13.

61 Ibid.

62 Ibid., pp. 13–14.

63 Ibid.

64 Mary O. Furner and Barry Supple, *The State and Economic Knowledge: The American and British Experiences* (Washington, DC: Woodrow Wilson International Center for Scholars and Cambridge University Press, 1990), pp. 15–16.

65 Ibid., p. 15.

66 Ibid.

67 Judith Goldstein and Robert O. Keohane, "Ideas and Foreign Policy," p. 10.

68 Peter Hall, "Policy Paradigms, Social Learning and the State: The Case of Economic Policy Making in Britain," *Comparative Politics* (1993), pp. 275–96. Peter Hall refers to the state-structural approach that recognizes the importance of societal forces in affecting state action. Social learning involves broad participation and conflict within the political system.

69 Andrew Britton, *Economic Policy Making in Britain 1974–1987* (New York: Cambridge University Press, 1991), pp. 134–5.

70 Ibid.

71 This is not to suggest, of course, that external forces dominate Britain's policy agenda. I brought out earlier that Britain's decision to withdraw from the ERM demonstrates a case that when "push comes to shove," Britain is quite capable of reasserting its monetary autonomy. The point here is simply that the United States and Britain differ in their exposure to international constraints.

72 Andrew Britton, *Economic Policy Making in Britain 1974–1987*, pp. 134–5.

73 Sven Steinmo, *Taxation and Democracy: Swedish, British, and American Approaches to Financing the Modern State* (New Haven: Yale University Press, 1993), p. 1.

74 Ibid., p. 3.

2 Paradigms, coalitions, and directional shifts in economic policy

1 Paul A. Sabatier, "Policy Change Over a Decade or More," in Paul A. Sabatier and Hank C. Jenkins Smith, eds, *Policy Change and Learning: An Advocacy Coalition Approach* (Boulder: Westview Press, 1993), p. 16.
2 Anthony E. Brown and Joseph Stewart Jr, "Competing Advocacy Coalitions, Policy Evaluation and Deregulation," in Paul A. Sabatier and Hank C. Jenkins Smith, eds, *Policy Change and Learning*, p. 101.
3 Paul A. Sabatier, "Policy Change Over a Decade or More," p. 29.
4 Paul A. Sabatier and Hank C. Jenkins Smith, "The Dynamics of Policy Oriented Learning," in Paul A. Sabatier and Hank C. Jenkins Smith, eds, *Policy Change and Learning*, p. 43.
5 See Theodore Lowi, "American Business, Public Policy, Case Studies, and Political Theory," *World Politics* 16 (1964), pp. 677–715.
6 Ibid.
7 Otto Singer, "Knowledge and Politics in Economic Policy-Making," in B. Guy Peters and Anthony Barker, eds, *Advising West European Governments: Inquiries, Expertise, and Public Policy* (Pittsburgh: University of Pittsburgh Press, 1993), p. 79.
8 Ibid.
9 Nicholas Henry, *Public Administration and Public Affairs*, 8th edn (New Jersey: Prentice Hall Press, 2001), p. 235.
10 Ibid.
11 Ibid.
12 Ibid.
13 Ibid.
14 Leroy N. Rieselbach, *Congressional Politics: The Evolving Legislative System* (Boulder: Westview Press, 1995), p. 335.
15 Ibid., p. 336.
16 Ibid., p. 337.
17 Ibid.
18 Norman C. Thomas, "Adapting Policy-Making Machinery to Fiscal Stress," in Harold D. Clarke, Marianne C. Stewart, and Gary Zuk, eds, *Economic Decline and Political Change: Canada, Great Britain, the United States* (Pittsburgh: Pittsburgh University Press, 1989), p. 41.
19 Otto Singer, "Knowledge and Politics in Economic Policy-Making," p. 81.
20 Ibid.
21 A.H. Halsey, "Commentary: From Welfare State to Post-Welfare Society," in Brian Brivati and Tim Bale, eds, *New Labour in Power: Precedents and Prospects* (London: Routledge, 1997), p. 62.
22 Nigel Lawson, *The View From Number 11: Britain's Longest Serving Cabinet Member Recalls the Triumphs and Disappointments of the Thatcher Era* (London: Doubleday Press, 1993), p. 985.
23 The Meade Report was drafted under the direction of Professor James Meade, the foremost exponent of the cause of switching to the VAT system.
24 Claudio M. Radaelli, "How Does Europeanization Produce Domestic Policy Change? Corporate Tax Policy in Italy and the United Kingdom," *Comparative Political Studies*, 30, No. 5 (October 1997), p. 566.
25 In 1983, the spending departments began working on a paper designed to encourage discussion of the various options and consequences for dealing with the public spending problem. Nigel Lawson objected to the original paper on the grounds that it was biased because the report was based exclusively on the Spending Departments' own estimates and spending aspirations. Under mounting pressure from the House of Commons Select Committee for the Treasury to publish a green paper on long-term public spending as a basis for public and parliamentary debate, Lawson presented his own green paper entitled

"The Next Ten Years: Public Expenditure and Taxation into the 1990s." The paper was comprehensive in scope and included the projected spending plans of the government until 1986–7. It included a discussion of the spending pressures in different sectors and the tax consequences of alternative spending trends and concluded that "Government and parliament must reach their judgement about what public expenditure in total can be afforded, then contain programs within that total." In the same way, Lawson subsequently published in 1986 a green paper entitled "The Reform of Personal Taxation." When examined together, these developments provide compelling evidence that tax and spending policies (even in the Thatcher era) were not created in a vacuum but rather included subsystem influences. See Nigel Lawson, *The View From Number 11*, pp. 304–5; 350–1; 596–7; 820–1.

26 Otto Singer, "Knowledge and Politics in Economic Policy-Making," pp. 76–9.

27 Ibid., p. 77.

28 Ibid., pp. 77–8.

29 Nigel Lawson set up an informal group of outside economists termed "gooies" (group of outside independent economists) who would meet periodically to offer advice on economic policy. Cited from Nigel Lawson, *The View From Number 11*, pp. 389–90.

30 Otto Singer, "Knowledge and Politics in Economic Policy-Making," p. 78.

31 Ibid., p. 78.

32 Ian Budge, Ivor Crewe, David McKay, and Ken Newton, *The New British Politics* (New York: Addison Wesley Longman, 1998), p. 256.

33 Ibid.

34 Ibid.

35 Ibid.

36 Ibid.

37 Over the period of March 1998–November 1999, I have interviewed several key members of this group who support this assertion.

38 *The Times*, 9 July 1999, p. 1.

39 Ibid.

40 *The Code for Fiscal Stability* is laid before Parliament under Section 155 of the Finance Act 1998.

41 HM Treasury document outlining *The Code For Fiscal Stability* (Royal Financial Print, 1998), p. 16.

42 Ibid.

43 This development further represents a major concession that [KWS] demand-management-led strategies can affect economic outcomes only in the short run and that sustainable growth can be generated only through market mechanisms.

44 Anil Hira, "How Ideas Affect Economic Policymaking in Developing Countries" [PhD dissertation], (Claremont: Claremont Graduate School, 1997), p. 312.

45 Martin Rein and Donald Schon, "Reframing Policy Discourse," in Frank Fischer and John Foster, eds, *The Argumentative Turn in Policy Analysis and Planning* (Durham: Duke University Press, 1993), p. 145.

46 Ibid., p. 157.

47 Ibid.

48 Ibid.

49 Ibid.

50 John F. Munro. "California Water Politics: Explaining Policy Change in a Cognitively Polarized Subsystem," in Paul A. Sabatier and Hank Jenkins-Smith, eds, *Policy Change and Learning*, p. 111.

51 Peter Hall, "Policy Paradigms, Social Learning, and the State: The Case of Economic Policymaking in Britain," *Comparative Politics* 25, No. 3 (April 1993), pp. 275–96, p. 280.

52 Patrick Akard. "The Return of the Market?: Reflections of the Real Conservative Tradition in US Policy Discourse," *Sociological Inquiry*, 65, No. 3–4 (1995), pp. 286–308, pp. 290–1.

53 Micheal J. Boskin, "Changing Views on the Changing Economy: The Alleged Crisis in Economics," in *Reagan and the Economy: The Success, Failures, and Unfinished Agenda* (San Francisco: ICS Press, 1987), p. 31. Demand management assumes that government has the ability to "fine tune the economy by constant adjustments in taxation, government spending, and the money supply ..."

54 This point was made by Lord Nigel Lawson in an interview that I had with him in London on November 24, 1998.

55 William Outhwaite and Tom Bottomore, eds, *The Blackwell Dictionary of Twentieth Century Social Thought* (Blackwell Reference, 1993), p. 129.

56 A.J. Weiner and H. Kahn, *Crisis and Arms Control* (Harmon-on-Hudson, NY: Hudson Institute, 1962), cited in David L. Sills, ed., *International Encyclopedia of the Social Sciences*, v. 3 (The Macmillan Company and the Free Press, 1968), pp. 510–11. Weiner and Kahn are cited for providing 12 generic dimensions of crises: "(1) Crisis is a turning point in an unfolding sequence of an event or action. (2) Crisis is a situation in which the requirement for action is high among participants. (3) Crisis threatens the goals and objectives of those involved. (4) Crisis followed by an important outcome whose consequences shape the future of the participants. (5) Crisis consists of a convergence of events that results in a new set of circumstances. (6) Crisis produces uncertainties in assessing a situation and in formulating alternatives for dealing with it. (7) Crisis reduces control over events and their effects. (8) Crisis heightens urgency, which often produces stress and anxiety among participants. (9) Crisis is a circumstance in which information available to participants is unusually inadequate. (10) Crisis increases time pressures for those involved. (11) Crisis is marked by changes in the relations among participants. (12) Crisis raises tensions among participants, especially in political crises involving nations."

57 See William Outwaite and Tom Bottomore, eds, *The Blackwell Dictionary of Twentieth-Century Thought*, p. 127.

58 Ibid., p. 129

59 Harold D. Clarke, Marianne C. Stewart, and Gary Zuk, "Introduction: Three Political Economies in an Era of Economic Decline," in Harold D. Clarke, Marianne C. Stewart, and Gary Zuk, eds, *Economic Decline and Political Change: Canada, Great Britain, the United States* (Pittsburgh: Pittsburgh University Press, 1989), p. 6.

60 Patrick Akard, "The Return of the Market?" p. 293.

61 Ibid.

62 Ibid.

63 Jack S. Levy, "Learning and Foreign Policy: Sweeping a Conceptual Minefield," in *International Organization,* 48, No. 2 (1994), pp. 279–312, p. 283.

64 Paul Sabatier and Hank Jenkins-Smith, "The Dynamics of Policy-Oriented Learning," p. 44.

65 Ibid., p. 42.

66 Ibid.

67 John F. Munro, "California Water Politics: Explaining Policy Change in a Cognitively Polarized System," p. 111.

68 Harold D. Clarke, Marianne C. Stewart, and Gary Zuk, "Introduction: Three Political Economies in an Era of Economic Decline," pp. 6–8.

69 Patrick Akard, "The Return of the Market?" p. 293.

70 Ibid., p. 294.

71 Ibid.

72 David Stoesz, *Small Change: Domestic Policy Under the Clinton Presidency* (New York: Longman Publishers, 1996), p. 12.

73 Ibid.

74 Ibid., pp. 12–13.

75 Ibid., p. 15.

76 Ibid.

77 Ibid., p. 17.

78 Ibid., p. 214.
79 Ibid., p. 180.
80 Ibid., p. 19.
81 Otto Singer, "Knowledge and Politics in Economic Policy-Making," p. 76.
82 Ibid., pp. 76–9.
83 Nigel Lawson, *The View From Number 11*, pp. 26–7. Margaret Thatcher used the term *dry* to apply to her core supporters and the term *wet* to apply to members in party who did not share her conviction or commitment for fiscal austerity.
84 Otto Singer, "Knowledge and Politics in Economic Policy-Making," p. 78.
85 Ibid., p. 77.
86 Ibid.
87 Ibid., p. 78.
88 Interview with Luke Bruce, Labour Party Policy Unit, July 21, 1999.
89 Commission on Social Justice, *Social Justice in a Changing World* (New York: IPPR, 1993), pp. 25–9.
90 Nick Ellison, *From Welfare State to Post-Welfare Society? Labour's Social Policy in Historical and Contemporary Perspective*, in Brian Brivati and Tim Bale, eds, *New Labour in Power: Precedents and Prospects* (London: Routledge Press, 1997), p. 52.
91 Ibid.
92 Ibid., p. 53.

3 Deficit reduction and tax reform in the Reagan–Thatcher era

1 Gary R. Evans, *Red Ink: The Budget Deficit, and Debt of the US Government* (San Diego: Academic Press, 1997), p. 34
2 Paul Pierson, *Dismantling the Welfare State: Reagan, Thatcher, and the Politics of Retrenchment* (Cambridge: Cambridge University Press, 1994), p. 34; R. Kent Weaver, "The Politics of Blame Avoidance," *Journal of Public Policy*, 6 (1986), pp. 371–96.
3 Paul Pierson, *Dismantling the Welfare State*, p. 34.
4 Gary R. Evans, *Red Ink*, p. 36.
5 Michal Boskin, *Reagan and the Economy: The Success, Failures, and Unfinished Agenda* (San Francisco: ICS Press, 1987), pp. 169–70; Margaret Thatcher, *The Downing Street Years* (New York: Harper Collins Press, 1993), p. 49.
6 Interview with Joe Grice, deputy director of Macroeconomic Policy and Prospects, HM Treasury, November 20, 1998.
7 Information about the United States cited from Gary R. Evans, *Red Ink*, p. 42; information about Britain cited from Margaret Thatcher, *The Downing Street Years*, pp. 50–1, and Geoffrey Howe, *Conflict of Loyalty* (London: Pan Books, 1995), p. 144.
8 William Niskanen, *Reaganomics: An Insider's Account of the Policies and the People* (New York: Oxford University Press, 1988), p. 25.
9 Ibid.
10 David Stockman, *The Triumph of Politics: How the Reagan Revolution Failed* (New York: Harper and Row, 1986), p. 353.
11 Michael J. Boskin, *Reagan and the Economy*, p. 171.
12 Nigel Lawson, *The View From Number 11: Britain's Longest Serving Cabinet Member Recalls the Triumphs and Disappointments of the Thatcher Era* (New York: Doubleday Press, 1993), p. 29.
13 Ibid., pp. 29–30.
14 Ibid., p. 70.
15 Gary R. Evans, *Red Ink*, p. 35.
16 James Miller III, *Fix the Budget: Urgings of an Abominable No-Man* (Stanford: Hoover Institution Press, 1994): 120–1.

17 Gregory B. Mills and John L. Palmer, *The Deficit Dilemma: Budget Policy in the Reagan Era* (Washington, DC: The Urban Institute Press, 1983), p. 5.
18 Ibid., pp. 5–6.
19 Michael Boskin, *Reagan and the Economy*, p. 2.
20 J. Harold McClure and Thomas D. Willett, "Understanding the Supply-Siders," in Craig Stubblebine and Thomas D. Willett, eds, *Reaganomics: A Midterm Report* (San Francisco: ICS Press, 1983), p. 60.
21 William Niskanen, *Reaganomics*, p. 5.
22 J. Harold McClure and Thomas D. Willett, "Understanding the Supply-Siders," p. 60.
23 William Niskanen, *Reaganomics*, p. 5.
24 Gregory B. Mills and John L. Palmer, *The Deficit Dilemma*, p. 17.
25 Ibid., p. 19.
26 William Niskanen, *Reaganomics*, p. 26.
27 Ibid.
28 Richard Fenno Jr., *The Emergence of a Senate Leader: Pete Domenici and the Reagan Budget* (Washington, DC: CQ Press, 1991), pp. 218–19.
29 See Michael Boskin, *Reagan and the Economy*, pp. 75–6.
30 James C. Miller III, *Fix the Budget: Urgings of an "Abominable No-Man,"* (Stanford: Hoover Institution Press, 1994), p. 30.
31 Ibid.
32 Ibid., p. 31.
33 David Stockman, *The Triumph of Politics*, p. 52.
34 Ibid.
35 Harry S. Havens, "Gramm–Rudman–Hollings: Origins and Implementation," *Public Budgeting and Finance* (Autumn 1986), pp. 4–24, p. 8.
36 Michael Boskin, *Reagan and the Economy*, p. 136.
37 Michael Meeropol, *Surrender: How the Clinton Administration Completed the Reagan Revolution* (Ann Arbor: University of Michigan Press, 1998): 123–4.
38 Harry S. Havens, "Gramm–Rudman–Hollings: Origins and Implementation," *Public Budgeting and Finance* (Autumn 1986), pp. 4–24, p. 9.
39 Ibid.
40 William Niskanen, *Reaganomics*, p. 26.
41 Ibid.
42 James Miller III, *Fix the US Budget*, pp. 34–5.
43 Daniel J. Miller, "The Grim Truth About Gramm–Rudman: The Deficit Law is Working," *Policy Review* (Spring 1990), pp. 76–9, pp. 76.
44 Ibid.
45 James Miller, III, *Fix the US Budget*, pp. 35.
46 Excerpt from the February 1990 Report by the Council of Economic Advisers. Cited in Michael Meeropol, *Surrender*, p. 132.
47 James Miller III, *Fix the US Budget*, p. 35.
48 Marvin H. Kosters, "Foreword," in Marvin H. Kosters, ed., *Fiscal Policies and the Budget Enforcement Act* (Washington, DC: AEI Press, 1992), p. ix.
49 Ibid.
50 Ibid.
51 James Edwin Kee and Scott V. Nystrom, "The 1990 Budget Package: Redefining The Debate," *Public Budgeting and Finance* (Spring 1991), pp. 3–24, p. 3.
52 Ibid., p. 8.
53 Rudolph G. Penner, "The Political Economics of the 1990 Budget Agreement," in Marvin H. Kosters, ed., *Fiscal Policies and the Budget Enforcement Act* (Washington, DC: AEI Press, 1992), p. 1.
54 William Niskanen, *Reaganomics*, p. 27.
55 Ibid.
56 Ibid.

57 Ibid., p. 106.
58 Michael Boskin, *Reagan and the Economy*, p. 2.
59 Ibid.
60 Ibid.
61 Nigel Lawson, *The View From Number 11*, p. 53.
62 Geoffrey Howe, *Conflict of Loyalty*, p. 161.
63 *Financial Times,* March 27, 1980, p. 1.
64 Margaret Thatcher, *The Downing Street Years*, p. 123.
65 Nigel Lawson, *The View From Number 11*, p. 53.
66 Ibid., p. 66.
67 Ibid., p. 67.
68 Alec Cairncross, *The British Economy Since 1945* (Oxford: Blackwell Publishers, 1992), p. 242.
69 Ibid.
70 The 1982 budget was introduced in the wake of massive unemployment. As a result, while fiscal policy remained restrictive, interest rates were allowed to fall slowly from October 1981 to November 1982. The 1983 budget was much like that of 1982.
71 Nigel Lawson brings out that this quote is the opening sentence of the Public Expenditure White Paper of November 1979. Cited from Nigel Lawson, *The View From Number 11*, p. 37.
72 Geoffrey Howe, *Conflict of Loyalty*, p. 172
73 Nigel Lawson, *The View From Number 11*, p. 283.
74 Alec Cairncross, *The British Economy Since 1945*, p. 250.
75 Ibid.
76 Ibid., p. 243.
77 Ibid.
78 Margaret Thatcher, *The Downing Street Years*, p. 123; and William Niskanen, *Reaganomics*, p. 27.
79 Alec Cairncross, *The British Economy Since 1945*, p. 265.
80 Ibid., p. 250.
81 Ibid.
82 Ibid., p. 264.
83 Ibid., p. 265.
84 Philip Norton, "The Lady's Not For Turning But What About the Rest?: Margaret Thatcher and the Conservative Party 1979–1989," *Parliamentary Affairs* (1990), p. 49.
85 Nigel Lawson, *The View From Number 11*, pp. 26–7.
86 Philip Norton, "The Lady's Not For Turning," p. 53.
87 Ibid.
88 Ibid., p. 49.
89 Ibid., pp. 49–50.
90 Ibid., p. 52.
91 Ibid., 49–50.
92 Ibid.
93 Ibid.
94 Ibid., p. 49.
95 Ibid.
96 Ibid., p. 50.
97 Ibid.
98 Ibid.
99 Nigel Lawson, *The View From Number 11*, p. 306.
100 Ibid., p. 300.
101 Ibid., p. 729.
102 Ibid.
103 Ibid., pp. 300–1.

104 Ibid., p. 301.
105 Ibid.
106 Ibid.
107 Ibid.
108 Ibid.
109 Ibid.
110 Ibid., pp. 301–2.
111 Ibid., p. 303.
112 Ibid.
113 Ibid.
114 Ibid.
115 Ibid.
116 Ibid.
117 Ibid., pp. 303–4.
118 Ibid., p. 304.
119 Ibid., pp. 308–9.
120 Ibid., p. 309.
121 Ibid.
122 Michael Boskin, *Reagan and the Economy*, p. 139.
123 Ibid.
124 Ibid.
125 Ibid.
126 Sven Steinmo, *Taxation and Democracy* (New Haven: Yale University Press, 1993), p. 171.
127 Ibid.
128 William Niskanen, *Reaganomics*, p. 71.
129 Ibid., p. 6.
130 Ibid., p. 106.
131 Ibid.
132 Ibid., pp. 74–5.
133 Ibid., p. 76.
134 Micheal Meeropol, *Surrender*, p. 106
135 William Niskanen, *Reaganomics*, pp. 76–7.
136 Ibid., p. 77.
137 Michael Boskin, *Reagan and the Economy*, p. 66.
138 William Niskanen, *Reaganomics*, pp. 85–6.
139 Micheal Meeropol, *Surrender*, p. 109.
140 Ibid., 109.
141 Michael J. Boskin, *Reagan and the Economy*, p. 86.
142 Ibid., p. 78.
143 William Niskanen, *Reaganomics*, p. 102.
144 Michael J. Boskin, *Reagan and the Economy*, p. 78.
145 Ibid., p. 80.
146 William Niskanen, *Reaganomics*, p. 84.
147 Ibid., pp. 84–5.
148 Nigel Lawson, *The View From Number 11*, p. 53.
149 Ibid., p. 35.
150 Margaret Thatcher, *The Downing Street Years*, pp. 42–3.
151 Nigel Lawson, *The View From Number 11*, p. 35.
152 Ibid., p. 32.
153 Ibid., p. 35.
154 Ibid.
155 "Dramatic Gains for the Rich," *Financial Times,* Wednesday, March 16, 1988, p. 25.
156 Sven Steinmo, *Taxation and Democracy*, (New Haven: Yale University Press, 1993), p. 172.

157 William Niskanen, *Reagonomics*, p. 86; Margaret Thatcher, *The Downing Street Years*, p. 43.
158 Sven Steinmo, *Taxation and Democracy*, p. 170
159 Ibid., p. 172.
160 Ibid., pp. 172–3.
161 Ibid., p. 174.
162 Ibid., pp. 174–5.
163 William Nikananen, *Reagonomics*, p. 86.
164 Nigel Lawson, *The View From Number 11*, p. 37.
165 William Niskanen, *Reagonomics*, p. 75.
166 Michael J. Boskin, *Reagan and the Economy*, p. 139
167 Sven Steinmo, *Taxation and Democracy*, p. 168.
168 Michael J. Boskin, *Reagan and the Economy*, p. 140.
169 Nigel Lawson, *The View From Number 11*, p. 72.

4 Deficit reduction and tax reform under Clinton and Blair

1 Thomas McLarty, *Preparing Our Country for the 21st Century: The Official Transcript of the United We Stand America Conference* (New York: Harper Perennial, 1995), p. 237.
2 Paul Pierson, "The Deficit and the Politics of Domestic Reform," in Margaret Weir, ed., *The Social Divide: Political Parties and the Future of Activist Government* (Washington, DC: Brookings Institution Press, 1998), p. 141.
3 CBO projections cited in *The Economist*, 7 February 1999, p. 27.
4 Desmond King and Mark Wickham-Jones, "From Clinton to Blair: The Democratic Party Origins of Welfare to Work," *Political Quarterly*, 70 (January–March 1999), pp. 62–74, pp. 64–5.
5 Ibid., p. 64.
6 Ibid.
7 Ibid.
8 "New Labour's Gurus: The American Connection," *The Economist*, November 8, 1997, p. 63.
9 Ibid.
10 *The Economist*, November 20, 1999, p. 30.
11 Ibid.
12 Ibid.
13 Bob Woodward, *The Agenda: Inside the Clinton White House* (New York: Simon and Schuster, 1994): 98. This was confirmed in an interview that I conducted with Lawrence Summers, April 23, 2001, The Brookings Institution.
14 Bob Woodward, *The Agenda*, p. 69.
15 Paul Pierson, "The Deficit and the Politics of Domestic Reform," p. 141.
16 Bob Woodward, *The Agenda*, p. 69.
17 Ibid.
18 Ibid.
19 Ibid.
20 Paul Pierson, "The Deficit and the Politics of Domestic Reform," p. 141.
21 Ibid., p. 144.
22 Ibid., p. 145.
23 Ibid., p. 128.
24 Ibid., p. 149.
25 Ibid., pp. 145–6.
26 Ibid.
27 Interview with Lawrence Summers, April 23, 2001, The Brookings Institution.

28 Ibid.
29 See Bob Woodward, *The Agenda*, pp. 97–8; interview with Ed Balls, November 18, 1998.
30 Bob Woodward, *The Agenda*, p. 69.
31 Martin Walker, *The President We Deserve: Bill Clinton, His Rise, Falls, and Comebacks* (New York: Crown Publishers, Inc, 1996), p. 169.
32 Ibid.
33 David Stoesz, *Small Change: Domestic Politics under the Clinton Presidency* (New York: Longman Publishers, 1996), p. 180.
34 Ibid., p. 179.
35 Michael Meeropol, *Surrender: How the Clinton Administration Completed the Reagan Revolution* (Ann Arbor: University of Michigan Press, 1998), p. 228.
36 Thomas McLarty, *Preparing Our Country for the 21st Century*, p. 237.
37 Martin Walker, *The President We Deserve*, p. 169.
38 Richard E. Cohen, "Special Report: The Splintered Congress," *National Journal*, 29 (January 25, 1997), pp. 154–62, pp. 159–60.
39 Ibid.
40 Paul Pierson, "The Deficit and the Politics of Domestic Reform," p. 127.
41 Desmond King and Mark Wickham-Jones, "From Clinton to Blair," p. 64.
42 Stanley B. Greenberg, *Middle Class Dreams: The Politics and Policy of a New American Majority* (New York: Times Books, 1995), p. 181.
43 See Thomas McLarty in Ross Perot, *Preparing Our Country for the 21st Century: The Official Transcript of the United We Stand America Conference*, p. 237.
44 Stanley B. Greenberg, *Middle Class Dreams*, p. 239.
45 Ibid.
46 Ibid.
47 Ibid., p. 208.
48 Ibid., p. 209.
49 Bob Woodward, *The Agenda*, p. 93.
50 Ibid.
51 Congressman John Kasich, "Options For Balancing the Federal Budget," in Ross Perot, ed., *Preparing Our Country for the 21st Century*, p. 67.
52 This group includes members from the East Coast, as well as Jim Moran, Virginia, the Midwest, Tin Roemer of Indiana and the West Coast, Calvin Dooley of California, that is dedicated to the cause of deficit reduction.
53 See Richard E. Cohen, "Special Report: The Splintered Congress," pp. 159–60.
54 Paul Pierson, "The Deficit and the Politics of Domestic Reform," p. 153.
55 Intervirew with Andrew Kilpatrick, Head of Macroeconomic and Fiscal Policy, HM Treasury, November 16, 1998; interview with Joe Grice, Head of Macroeconomic Policy and Prospects, HM Treasury, November 20, 1998.
56 Nick Ellison, "From Wefare State to Post Welfare Society: Labour's Social Policy in Historical Perspective," in Brian Brivati and Tim Bale, eds, *New Labour in Power: Precedents and Prospects*, p. 48.
57 Interview with Andrew Kilpatrick, Head of Macroeconomic and Fiscal Policy, HM Treasury, November 16, 1998.
58 Stephen Driver and Luke Martell, *New Labour: Politics After Thatcherism* (Oxford: Blackwell Publishers, 1998): 76.
59 Based on the US model, workfare entailed a direct link between assistance for the unemployed and individual responsibility. It involved an interventionist strategy that would provide, above all, the means to provide unemployed individuals with education and skills training to meet the new demands imposed by an increasingly competitive labor market.
60 Stephen Driver and Luke Martell, *New Labour*, p. 75.
61 Interview with Ed Balls, Special Economic Adviser to Gordon Brown, Chancellor of the Exchequer, HM Treasury, November 18, 1998.

62 Desmond King and Mark Wickham-Jones, "From Clinton to Blair," pp. 65–6.
63 Ibid.
64 Interview with Ed Balls, Special Adviser to the Chancellor of the Exchequer, HM Treasury, November 18, 1998.
65 Interview with Andrew Kilpatrick. Head of Macroeconomic and Fiscal Policy, HM Treasury, November 16, 1998.
66 Stephen Driver and Luke Martell, *New Labour*, p. 25.
67 Interview with Ed Balls, Special Adviser to the Chancellor of the Exchequer, HM Treasury, November 18, 1998.
68 *The Economist*, "New Labour's Gurus," November 8, 1997, p. 63.
69 Ibid.
70 Interview with Ed Balls, Special Adviser to the Chancellor of the Exchequer, HM Treasury, November 18, 1998; Interview with Lawrence Summers, Brookings Institution, April 23, 2001.
71 Interview with Andrew Kilpatrick, Head of Macroeconomic and Fiscal Policy, HM Treasury, November 16, 1998.
72 Simon Lee, "The Political Economy of the Third Way," paper presented at the Global Turbulence: Crisis in National and International Political Economy Conference, Simon Fraser University, July 2001, p. 3.
73 Ibid.
74 Ibid., p. 5.
75 Ibid.
76 Ibid.
77 Interview with Joe Grice, Deputy Director, Macroeconomic Policy and Prospects, November 20, 1998.
78 See Stephen Driver and Luke Martell, *New Labour: Politics After Thatcherism*, pp. 41–2.
79 Interview with Andrew Maugham, Special Adviser to the Chief Secretary, HM Treasury, March 19, 1998.
80 *Financial Times*, "The Chancellor of the Exchequer's Budget Statement," March 16, 1999, p. 1.
81 Ibid.
82 *Financial Times*, March 18, 1998, p. 22
83 Stephen Driver and Luke Martell, *New Labour*, p. 64.
84 Interview with Luke Bruce, The Labour Party Policy Unit, Milbank Tower, July 21, 1999.
85 *Financial Times*, March 18, 1998, p. 22.
86 Stephen Driver and Luke Martell, *New Labour: Politics After Thatcherism*, p. 63.
87 Interview with Andrew Kilpatrick, Head of Macroeconomic Policy and Prospects, HM Treasury, November 16, 1998.
88 Stephen Driver and Luke Martell, *New Labour*, p. 63.
89 *Financial Times*, March 18, 1998, p. 3.
90 Ibid.
91 Ibid., p. 1.
92 Interview with Andrew Kilpatrick, July 20, 1999.
93 Simon Lee, "The Political Economy of the Third Way," p. 4.
94 Ibid.
95 Ibid.
96 Ibid.
97 Ibid.
98 Ibid.
99 Ibid.
100 Ibid.
101 Ibid., p. 9.
102 Ibid., p. 7.
103 Ibid.

104 Ibid.
105 Ibid.
106 Ibid., p. 8.
107 Stanley B. Greenberg, *Middle Class Dreams*, pp. 43–4; Martin Walker, *The President We Deserve*, p. 353; Bob Woodward, *The Agenda*, p. 243; interview with Andrew Kilpatrick, Head of Macroeconomic and Fiscal Policy, HM Treasury, November 16, 1998.
108 *The Economist*, "New Labour's Gurus," p. 63
109 Interview with Andrew Kilpatrick, Head Macroeconomic and Fiscal Policy, HM Treasury, November 16, 1998.
110 *The Economist*, "New Labour's Gurus," p. 63.
111 Interview with Andrew Kilpatrick, November 16, 1998.
112 *The Economist*, "New Labour's Gurus," p. 63
113 Michael Meeropol, *Surrender*, p. 1.
114 Senator Pete Domenici, "The Need To Balance the Federal Budget," in Ross Perot, ed., *Preparing Our Country for the 21st Century: The Official Transcript of the United We Stand Conference* (New York: Harper Perennial, 1995): 52–8.
115 *Congressional Quarterly*, June 3, 1995, p. 1563.
116 *Congressional Quarterly*, June 17, 1995, p. 1718
117 Ibid.
118 Ibid.
119 Ibid., p. 1716.
120 Ibid., p. 1718
121 Michael Meeropol, *Surrender*, p. 2
122 Ibid.
123 Ibid.
124 *Congressional Quarterly*, October 5, 1996, p. 2826.
125 Michael Meeropol, *Surrender*, p. 228
126 Ibid., pp. 228–9.
127 White House press release, October 30, 2000.
128 'The Clinton budget: the impact on key agencies', *The Wall Street Journal*, February 6, 1997, pp. A12–13.
129 Michael Meeropol, *Surrender*, p. 1
130 *Congressional Quarterly*, August 3, 1996, pp. 2175–6.
131 Michael Meeropol, *Surrender*, p. 1
132 Ibid., p. 6.
133 Ibid.
134 *Congressional Quarterly*, August 3, 1996, p. 2175
135 Ibid.
136 Congressional Quarterly, September 21, 1996, pp. 2705–6.
137 *Congressional Quarterly*, August 3, 1996, p. 2175
138 *Congressional Quarterly*, February 8, 1998, p. 332.
139 Ibid.
140 Ibid., p. 333.
141 Ibid.
142 *The Economist*, March 21, 1998, p. 41
143 Ibid.
144 Ibid.
145 Ibid., p. 36.
146 Ibid.
147 Ibid.
148 Ibid.
149 Ibid.
150 Ibid.
151 Interview with Ed Balls, November 18, 1998.

152 Ibid.
153 *The Economist*, March 21, 1998, p. 36
154 Ibid., p. 41.
155 Ibid., p. 36.
156 William Niskanen, *Reganomics*, p. 286; interview with the Rt. Hon. the Lord Nigel Lawson of Blaby, Central European Trust, Knightsbridge, November 24, 1998.
157 Paul A. Sabatier, "Policy Change Over a Decade or More," in Paul A. Sabatier and Hank C. Jenkins-Smith, eds, *Policy Change and Learning: An Advocacy Coalition Approach* (Boulder: Westview Press, 1993), p. 16.
158 Ibid.

5 Summary

1 Geoffrey Garrett and Peter Lange, What's Left for the Left?" *International Organization* 45, No. 4 (1991), pp. 539–64.
2 Coalitions may attempt to go "venue shopping."
3 Anthony E. Brown and Joseph Stewart Jr, "Competing Advocacy Coalitions, Policy Evaluation and Deregulation," in Paul A. Sabatier and Hank C. Jenkins Smith, eds, *Policy Change and Learning*, p. 101.
4 Paul A. Sabatier, "Policy Change Over a Decade or More," p. 22.
5 Patrick Akard. "The Return of the Market?" *Sociological Inquiry*, 65, No. 3–4 (1995), pp. 286–308, pp. 290–1.
6 Micheal J. Boskin, "Changing Views on the Changing Economy," in *Reagan and the Economy*, p. 31. "Demand management assumes that government has the ability to "fine tune the economy by constant adjustments in taxation, government spending, and the money supply ..."
7 See William Outwaite and Tom Bottomore, eds, *The Blackwell Dictionary of Twentieth-Century Thought*, p. 127.
8 David Stoesz, *Small Change*, pp. 12–13.
9 Otto Singer, "Knowledge and Politics in Economic Policy-Making," in B. Guy Peters and Anthony Barker, eds, *Advising West European Governments*, p. 79.
10 Otto Singer, "Knowledge and Politics in Economic Policy-Making," p. 81.
11 Ibid., pp. 77–8.
12 Nigel Lawson set up an informal group of outside economists termed 'gooies' (group of outside independent economists) who would meet periodically to offer advice on economic policy. Cited from Nigel Lawson, *The View From Number 11*, pp. 389–90.
13 Paul Pierson, *Dismantling the Welfare State*, p. 34; R. Kent Weaver, "The Politics of Blame Avoidance," *Journal of Public Policy*, 6 (1986), pp. 371–96.
14 Paul Pierson, *Dismantling the Welfare State*, p. 34.
15 Michael J. Boskin, *Reagan and the Economy*, p. 171.
16 Gary R. Evans, *Red Ink*, p. 35
17 James Miller III, *Fix the Budget*, pp. 120–1.
18 Margaret Thatcher, *The Downing Street Years*, p. 123.
19 Nigel Lawson, *The View From Number 11*, p. 53.
20 William Niskanen, *Reaganomics*, p. 27; Margaret Thatcher, *The Downing Street Years*, pp. 50–1.
21 Nigel Lawson, *The View From Number 11*, pp. 31–2; William Niskanen, *Reaganomics*, p. 23.
22 Alec Cairncross, *The British Economy Since 1945*, p. 249
23 Ibid.
24 William Niskanen, *Reaganomics*, pp. 108–9.
25 Gregory B. Mills and John L. Palmer, *The Deficit Dilemma*, p. 17; William Niskanen, *Reagonomics*, p. 106.

26　Ibid., p. 172.
27　Interview with Andrew Kilpatrick. Head of Macroeconomic and Fiscal Policy, HM Treasury, November 16, 1998.
28　Bob Woodward, *The Agenda*, p. 98.
29　*The Economist*, December 14–20, 2002.
30　*The Economist*, July 27–August 2, 2002, pp. 27–8.
31　Ibid.
32　*The Economist*, June 22–28, 2002.
33　Ibid.
34　Ibid., pp. 27–8.
35　Ibid.
36　*The Economist*, December 14–20, 2002.
37　Ibid.
38　Ibid.
39　Ibid.
40　Ibid.
41　Peter G. Gosselin, "Friedman Appointment as Bush Advisor Put Off for a 2nd Day," *L. A. Times*, December 11, 2000.
42　Ibid.
43　Ibid.
44　Ibid.
45　*The Economist*, November 30–December 6, 2002, pp. 13–14.
46　Ibid.
47　Ibid.
48　Ibid.
49　Ibid.

Bibliography

Akard, Patrick. "The Return of the Market?: Reflections of the Real Conservative Tradition in US Policy Discourse," *Sociological Inquiry*, 65, No. 3–4 (1995), pp. 286–308, pp. 290–1.

Andrews, David. "Capital Mobility and State Autonomy: Toward a Structural Theory of International Monetary Relations," *International Studies Quarterly*, 38, No. 2 (June 1994), pp. 193–218.

Andrews, David and Willett, Thomas. "Financial Interdependence and the State: International Monetary Relations at Century's End," *International Organization*, 51 (1997), pp. 479–511.

Axelrod, Robert, ed. *The Structure of Decision*. Princeton: Princeton University Press, 1976.

Barker, Rodney, ed. "Political Ideas and Political Action." *Political Studies*, 48, Special Issue 20, March 21, 2001, pp. 221–387.

Baumgartner, Frank R. and Jones, Bryan D. *Agendas and Instability in American Politics*. Chicago: The University of Chicago Press, 1993.

Bennett, Michael and Howlett, Colin J. "The Lessons of Learning: Reconciling Theories of Policy Learning and Policy Change." *Policy Sciences*, 25 (1992), pp. 275–94.

Bessette, Joseph M. *The Mild Voice of Reason: Deliberative Democracy and American National Government*. Chicago: Chicago University Press, 1994.

Blake, Robert. *The Conservative Party From Peel to Major*. London: William Heinemann, 1997 rev. edn.

Blank, Stephen. "Britain: The Politics of Foreign Economic Policy, the Domestic Economy, and the Problem of Pluralistic Stagnation." *International Organization*, 31 (1977), pp. 673–721.

Blustein, Paul. "What's In Demand? Supply-Siders Are, For Economic Ideas; Their Consulting Firms Gain, And So Does Infighting." *Wall Street Journal*, October 12, 1981, p. 198.

Boskin, Michael J. *Reagan and the Economy: The Successes, Failures, and Unfinished Agenda*. San Francisco: ICS Press, 1987.

Boyle, Nigel. *Crafting Change: Labor Market Policy Under Mrs. Thatcher* (forthcoming).

Britton, Andrew. *Economic Policy Making in Britain 1974–1987*. New York: Cambridge University Press, 1991.

Brivati, Brian and Bale, Tim, eds. *New Labour in Power: Precedents and Prospects*. London: Routledge, 1997.

Brown, Anthony E. and Stewart, Joseph Jr. "Competing Advocacy Coalitions, Policy Evaluation and Deregulation," in Paul A. Sabatier and Hank C. Jenkins Smith, eds. *Policy Change and Learning: An Advocacy Coalition Approach*. Boulder: Westview Press, 1993.

Budge, Ian, Crewe, Ivor, McKay, Davis, and Newton, Ken. *The New British Politics*. New York: Addison Wesley Longman, 1998.

Business Week. "A Guide to Understanding the Supply-Siders: Resurrecting Classical Theories on Supply, Demand, and Tax Cuts [ideas underlying President-Elect Ronald Reagan's economic program]." December 22, 1980, pp. 75–8.

Cairncross, Alec. *The British Economy Since 1945*. Oxford: Blackwell Publishers, 1992.

Campbell, John. "Unclogging Britain's Arteries: Economic Growth Has Overwhelmed Britain" Road Network; The Government Is Fighting Back With Money—and New Ideas." *Investors Chronicle*, 88 (June 23, 1989), pp. 20–2.

"The Chancellor of the Exchequer's Budget Statement." *Financial Times*, March 16, 1999, p. 1.

Clarke, Harold D., Stewart, Marianne C., and Zuk, Gary, eds. *Economic Decline and Political Change: Canada, Great Britain, the United States*. Pittsburgh: Pittsburgh University Press, 1989.

Cohen, Richard E. "Special Report: The Splintered Congress," *National Journal*, January 25, 1997, pp. 154–69.

Colander, David C., and Coats, A.W., eds. *The Spread of Economic Ideas*. New York: Cambridge University Press, 1989.

Congressional Quarterly, December 31, 1994, p. 3601.

Congressional Quarterly, June 3, 1995, p. 1563.

Congressional Quarterly, June 17, 1995, p. 1718.

Congressional Quarterly, December 17, 1995, p. 3560.

Congressional Quarterly, August 3, 1996, p. 2175.

Congressional Quarterly, September 21, 1996, pp. 2705–6.

Congressional Quarterly, October 5, 1996, p. 2826.

Congressional Quarterly, February 8, 1998, pp. 332–3.

Crafts, Nicholas. *The Conservative Government's Economic Record: An End of Term Report. Institute of Economic Affairs*, 1998.

Cranford, John C. "Economic Policy: Bush's Plan Consolidates, Recycles Old Ideas." *Congressional Quarterly Weekly Report*, 50, September 12, 1992, p. 2705.

Deacon, Alan. "Learning From The US? The Influence of American Ideas Upon "New Labour" Thinking on Welfare Reform." *Policy and Politics*, 28, No. 1 (January 2000), pp. 5–18.

Denzau, Arthur T., and North, Douglas C. "Shared Mental Models: Ideologies and Institutions," *KyKlos*, 47, 1994, pp. 3–31.

Douglas, Mary. *How Institutions Think*. Syracuse: Syracuse University, 1986.

Downs, Anthony. *An Economic Theory of Democracy*. New York: Harper and Row, 1957.

Driver, Stephen, and Martell, Luke. *New Labour: Politics After Thatcherism*. Oxford: Blackwell Publishers, 1998.

Dutton, David. *British Politics Since 1945: The Rise, Fall And Rebirth of Consensus*, 2nd edn. Oxford: Blackwell Publishers, 1997.

The Economist, "What Now?" 331, May 14, 1994, p. 57.

The Economist, "New Labour's Gurus: The American Connection." November 8, 1997, p. 63.

The Economist, March 21, 1998, p. 41.

The Economist, November 20, 1999, p. 30.

The Economist, "The Hardest Act to Follow," 355, No. 8172 (May 27, 2000), p. 62.

The Economist, "Back to Class War," 355, No. 8173 (June 3, 2000), pp. 55–8.

The Economist, June 9, 2001, p. 10.

The Economist, "Fiscal Policy: A Decade of Deficits," 363, No. 8278 (June 22, 2002), pp. 27–8.

The Economist, "George Bush: The Disappearing Presidency," 364, No. 8283 (July 27, 2002), pp. 27–8.

The Economist, "There's Nothing Like An Enemy: Beating the Firemen is a Necessary But Not Sufficient Answer to Union Militancy." 365, No. 8301 (November 30, 2002), 50.

The Economist, "Britain's Public Finances: The Bill to Come." 365, No. 8301 (November 30, 2002), pp. 13–14.

The Economist, "A Tale of Two Legacies: Why Are The Heirs of Ronald Reagan Doing So Much Better Than Margaret Thatcher's." 365, No. 8304 (December 21, 2002), pp. 64–6.

Ellison, Nick. "From Welfare State to Post-Welfare Society? Labour's Social Policy in Historical and Contemporary Perspective," in Brian Brivati and Tim Bale, eds. *New Labour in Power: Precedents and Prospects*. London: Routledge Press, 1997.

Evans, Gary R. *Red Ink: The Budget Deficit, and Debt of the US Government*. San Diego: Academic Press, 1997.

Fenno, Richard Jr. *The Emergence of a Senate Leader: Pete Domenici and the Reagan Budget*. Washington, DC: CQ Press, 1991.

Financial Times, March 27, 1980, p. 1.

Financial Times, "Dramatic Gains for the Rich," March 16, 1988, p. 23.

Financial Times, March 18, 1998, p. 22.

Furner, Mary O., and Supple, Barry. *The State and Economic Knowledge: The American and British Experiences*. Washington, DC: Woodrow Wilson International Center for Scholars and Cambridge University Press, 1990.

Gamble, Andrew. *Britain in Decline: Economic Policy, Political Strategy and The British State*, 4th edn. Macmillan Publishers and St Martin's Press, 1994.

Gamble, Andrew. *Hayek: The Iron Cage of Liberty*. Boulder: Westview Press, 1996.

Garrett, Geoffrey. "Capital Mobility, Trade, and Domestic Politics," in Robert O. Keohane and Helen V. Milner, eds. *Internationalization and Domestic Politics*. Cambridge: Cambridge University Press, 1996.

Garrett, Geoffrey. *Partisan Politics in the Global Economy*. New York: Cambridge University Press, 1998.

Garrett, Geoffrey and Lange, Peter. "What's Left for the Left?" *International Organization* 45, No. 4 (1991), pp. 539–64.

Gelb, Norman. "Polarizing British Politics: Bournemouth vs. Blackpool." *New Leader*, 82, No. 13 (November 1–15, 1999), pp. 9–10.

Geyer, Robert. "Globalization and the (Non)-Defense of the Welfare State." *West European Politics*, 121, No. 3 (1998), pp. 77–102.

Goldstein, Judith. "The Political Economy of Trade: Institutions of Protection." *American Political Science Review*, 80, No. 1 (1986), pp. 180–1.

Goldstein, Judith, and Keohane, Robert O. "Ideas and Foreign Policy: An Analytic Framework," in Judith Goldstein and Robert O. Keohane, eds. *Ideas and Foreign Policy: Beliefs, Institutions, and Political Change*. Ithaca: Cornell University Press, 1993.

Goodman, John, and Pauly, Louis. "The Obsolescence of Capital Controls? Economic Management in an Age of Global Markets." *World Politics*, 46 (1993), pp. 50–82.

Gosselin, Peter G. "Friedman Appointment as Bush Advisor Put Off for a second Day." *L. A. Times*, December 11, 2002, p. A1.

Gourevitch, Peter. *Politics in Hard Times: Comparative Responses to International Economic Crises*. Ithaca: Cornell University Press, 1986.

Greenaway, John. *Deciding Factors in British Politics: A Case-Studies Approach*. London: Routledge, 1992.

Greenberg, Stanley B. *Middle Class Dreams: The Politics and Policy of a New American Majority*. New York: Times Books, 1995.

Haas, Earnest B. *When Knowledge is Power: Three Models of Change in International Organization*. Los Angeles: University of California Press, 1990.

Haas, Peter, ed. "1992 Special Edition on Epistemic Communities." *International Organization*, 46, No. 1 (1992).

Hall, Peter. "Policy Paradigms, Social Learning, and the State: The Case of Economic Policymaking in Britain." *Comparative Politics*, 25, No. 3 (April 1993), pp. 275–96.

Hall, Peter. *The Political Power of Economic Ideas: Keynesianism Across Nations*. Princeton: Princeton University Press, 1989.

Hallerberg, Mark, and Clark, William Roberts. "How Should Political Scientists Measure Capital Mobility? A Review." Paper prepared for presentation at the 1997 Annual Meeting of the American Political Science Association, Washington, DC, August 28–31.

Halsey, A.H. "Commentary: From Welfare State to Post-Welfare Society," in Brian Brivati and Tim Bale, eds. *New Labour in Power: Precedents and Prospects*. London: Routledge, 1997.

Harris, Robin, ed. *The Collected Speeches of Margaret Thatcher*. New York: Harper Collins Publishers, 1997.

Havens, Harry S. "Gramm–Rudman–Hollings: Origins and Implementation." *Public Budgeting and Finance* (Autumn 1986), 4–24.

Helleiner, Eric. *States and the Reemergence of Global Finance: From Bretton Woods to the 1990s*. Ithaca: Cornell University Press, 1994.

Henry, Nicholas. *Public Administration and Public Affairs*, 8th edn. Englewood Cliffs, NJ: Prentice Hall Press, 2001.

Hira, Anil. "How Ideas Affect Economic Policymaking in Developing Countries" [PhD dissertation]. Claremont: Claremont Graduate School, 1997.

HM Treasury document outlining the *Code For Fiscal Stability*. London: Royal Financial Print, 1998.

Hoskyns, John. *Just in Time: Inside The Thatcher Revolution*. Aurum Press, 2000.

Howe, Geoffrey. *Conflict of Loyalty*. London: Pan Books, 1995.

Jacobsen, John Kurt. "Much Ado About Ideas," in *Dead Reckonings: Ideas, Interests, and Politics in the "Information Age."* Atlantic Highlands, NJ: Humanities Press International, 1997.

Janis, Irving L. *Groupthink: Psychological Studies of Policy Decisions and Fiascoes*. Boston: Houghton Mifflin, 1982.

Jenkins, Simon. *Accountable to None: The Tory Nationalization of Britain*. London: Hamish Hamilton, 1995.

Jowell, Roger, Curtice, John, Park, Alison, Brook, Lindsay, Thomson, Katarina, and Bryson, Caroline, eds. *British Social Attitudes: The 14th Report: The End of Conservative Values*. Aldershot: Ashgate Publishing Company, 1997.

Kee, Edwin James, and Nystrom, Scott V. "The 1990 Budget Package: Redefining The Debate," *Public Budgeting and Finance*, Spring 1991, pp. 3–24.

King, Desmond, and Wickham-Jones, Mark. "From Clinton to Blair: The Democratic Party Origins of Welfare to Work." *Political Quarterly*, 70 (January–March 1999), pp. 62–74.

Knoke, David. *Political Networks: The Structural Perspective*. New York: Cambridge University Press, 1990.

Kosters, Marvin H., ed. *Fiscal Policies and the Budget Enforcement Act*. Washington, DC: AEI Press, 1992.

Kuhn, Thomas. *The Structure of Scientific Revolutions*. Chicago: University of Chicago Press, 1970.

Kurzer, Paulette. *Business and Banking: Political Change and Economic Integration in Western Europe*. Ithaca: Cornell University Press, 1993.

Lawson, Nigel. *The View From Number 11: Britain's Longest Serving Cabinet Member Recalls the Triumphs and Disappointments of the Thatcher Era*. London: Doubleday Press, 1993.

Lee, Simon. "The Political Economy of the Third Way." Paper presented at the Global Turbulence: Crisis in National and International Political Economy Conference, Simon Fraser University, July, 2001

Levy, Jack S. "Learning and Foreign Policy: Sweeping a Conceptual Minefield." *International Organization*, 48, No. 2 (1994), pp. 279–312.

Lindblom, Charles E. "The Science of Muddling Through." *Public Administration Review*, 19 (1959), pp. 79–88.

Lipset, Seymour Martin. "What Are Parties For?" *Journal of Democracy*, 7, No. 1 (1996), pp. 169–75.

Lowi, Theodore. "American Business, Public Policy, Case Studies, and Political Theory." *World Politics*, 16 (1964), pp. 687–91.

Malabre, Alfred L. Jr. "May His Ideas Rest In Peace [influence of Milton Friedman's economic ideas on the domestic and international economic scene]." *Wall Street Journal*, 190, November 17, 1977, 28,

Mansbridge, Jane J. *Beyond Self Interest*. Chicago: University of Chicago Press, 1990.

McClure, Harold J., and Willett, Thomas D. "Understanding the Supply-Siders," in Stubblebine, Craig and Willett, Thomas D., eds. *Reaganomics: A Midterm Report*. San Francisco: ICS Press, 1983.

McGann, James G., and Weaver, R. Kent, eds. *Think Tanks and Civil Societies: Catalysts For Ideas and Action*. New Brunswick: Transaction Publishers, 2000.

The McGraw-Hill Dictionary of Modern Economics. New York: McGraw-Hill, 1983.

McLarty, Thomas. *Preparing Our Country of the 21st Century: The Official Transcript of the United We Stand America Conference*. New York: Harper Perennial, 1995.

Meeropol, Michael. *Surrender: How the Clinton Administration Completed the Reagan Revolution*. Ann Arbor: University of Michigan Press, 1998.

Miller, Daniel J. "The Grim Truth About Gramm–Rudman: The Deficit Law is Working." *Policy Review*, Spring 1990, pp. 76–80.

Miller, James III. *Fix the US Budget: Urgings of an Abominable No-Man*. Stanford: Hoover Institution Press, 1994.

Mills, Gregory B., and Palmer, John L. *The Deficit Dilemma: Budget Policy in the Reagan Era*. Washington, DC: The Urban Institute Press, 1983.

Munro, John F. "California Water Politics: Explaining Policy Change in a Cognitively Polarized System," in Paul A. Sabatier and Hank C. Jenkins Smith, eds. *Policy Change and Learning: An Advocacy Coalition Approach*. Boulder: Westview Press, 1993.

Nell, Edward. *Free Market Conservatism: A Critique of Theory and Practice*. London: George Allen and Unwin, 1984.

Niskanen, William. *Reaganomics: An Insider's Account of the People and Policies*. New York: Oxford University Press, 1988.

Norton, Philip. "The Lady's Not For Turning But What About the Rest?: Margaret Thatcher and the Conservative Party 1979–1989," *Parliamentary Affairs* (1990), p. 49.

Notermans, Ton. "The Abdication of National Policy Autonomy." *Politics and Society*, (1993), 21 (June), pp. 133–67.

Outhwaite, William, and Bottomore, Tom, eds. *The Blackwell Dictionary of Twentieth Century Social Thought*. London: Blackwell Reference, 1993.

Parker, M.J. *Thatcherism and The Fall of Coal*. New York: Oxford University Press, 2000.

Pauly, Louis. *Opening Financial Markets: Banking Politics on the Pacific Rim*. Ithaca: Cornell University Press, 1998.

Penner, Rudolph G. "The Political Economics of the 1990 Budget Agreement," in Marvin H. Kosters, ed. *Fiscal Policies and the Budget Enforcement Act*. Washington, DC: AEI Press, 1992.

Perot, Ross *Preparing Our Country for the 21st Century: The Official Transcript of the "United We Stand America" Conference*. New York: Harper Perennial, p. 67.

Peters, B. Guy and Barker, Anthony, eds. *Advising West European Governments: Inquiries, Expertise, and Public Policy*. Pittsburgh: University of Pittsburgh Press, 1993.

Pierson, Paul. *Dismantling the Welfare State: Reagan, Thatcher, and the Politics of Retrenchment*. Cambridge: Cambridge University Press, 1994.

Pierson, Paul. "The Deficit and Politics of Domestic Reform," in Margaret Weir, ed. *The Social Divide: Political Parties and the Future of Activist Government*. Washington, DC: Brookings Institution Press, 1998.

Porter, Glenn, ed. *Encyclopedia of American Economic History: Studies of The Principal Movements and Ideas*. 3 vols. New York: Macmillan, 1980.

Radaelli, Claudio M. "How Does Europeanization Produce Domestic Policy Change? Corporate Tax Policy in Italy and the United Kingdom." *Comparative Political Studies*, 30, No. 5 (October 1997), pp. 553–75.

Rein, Martin, and Schon, Donald. "Reframing Policy Discourse," in Frank Fischer and John Foster, eds., *The Argumentative Turn in Policy Analysis and Planning*. Durham: Duke University Press, 1993.

Reitan, Earl A. *Tory Radicalism: Margaret Thatcher, John Major, and The Transformation of Modern Britain, 1979–1997*. Lanham: Rowman & Littlefield Publishers, Inc., 1997.

Rieselbach, Leroy N. *Congressional Politics: The Evolving Legislative System*. Boulder: Westview Press, 1995.

Riker, William. *The Art of Political Manipulation*. New York: Yale University Press, 1986.

Rogowski, Ronald. *Commerce and Coalitions: How Trade Affects Domestic Political Alignments*. Princeton: Princeton University Press, 1989.

Ruggie, John. "International Regimes, Transactions, and Change: Embedded Liberalism the postwar Economic Order." *International Organization*, 36, No. 2 (1982), pp. 382–415.

Sabatier, Paul A. "Policy Change Over a Decade or More," in Paul A. Sabatier and Hank C. Jenkins-Smith, eds. *Policy Change and Learning: An Advocacy Coalition Approach*. Boulder: Westview Press, 1993.

Sabatier, Paul A., and Jenkins Smith, Hank C. "The Dynamics of Policy Oriented Learning," in Paul A. Sabatier and Hank C. Jenkins Smith, eds. *Policy Change and Learning: An Advocacy Coalition Approach*. Boulder: Westview Press, 1993.

Sabatier, Paul and Pelkey, Neil. "Incorporating Multiple Actors and Guidance Instruments into Models of Regulatory Policymaking: An Advocacy Coalition Framework," *Administration and Society*, 19 (1987), pp. 236–63.

Scharpf, Fritz. *Crisis and Choice in European Social Democracy*. Ithaca: Cornell University Press, 1991.

Singer, Otto. "Knowledge and Politics in Economic Policy-Making: Official Economic Advisers in the USA, Great Britain, Germany," in B. Guy Peters and Anthony Barker, eds. *Advising West European Governments: Inquiries, Expertise, and Public Policy*. Pittsburgh: University of Pittsburgh Press, 1993.

Stein, Herbert. "The Chief Executive as the Chief Economist," in *Washington Bed Time Stories: The Politics of Money and Jobs*. New York: The Free Press, 1986.

Stein, Herbert, *Presidential Economics: The Making of Economic Policy from Roosevelt to Clinton*. Washington, DC: American Enterprise Institute Press, 1994.

Steinmo, Sven. *Taxation and Democracy: Swedish, British, and American Approaches to Financing the Modern State*. New Haven: Yale University Press, 1993.

Stockman, David. *The Triumph of Politics: How the Reagan Revolution Failed*. New York: Harper and Row, 1986.

Stoesz, David. *Small Change: Domestic Politics Under the Clinton Presidency*. New York: Longman Publishers, 1996.

Stone, Debrah. *Policy Paradox and Political Reason*. New York: HarperCollins Publishers, 1988.

Stephens, Phillip. *Politics and The Pound: The Conservatives' Struggle With Sterling*. London: Macmillan; Trans-Atlantic Publications, 1996.

Taylor, Robert. *The Trade Union Question in British Politics: Government and Unions Since 1945*. London: Blackwell Publishers, 1993.

Thatcher, Margaret, *The Downing Street Years*. London: HarperCollins, 1994.

Thomas, Norman C. "Adapting Policy-Making Machinery to Fiscal Stress," in Harold D. Clarke, Marianne C. Stewart, and Gary Zuk, eds. *Economic Decline and Political Change: Canada, Great Britain, the United States*. Pittsburgh: Pittsburgh University Press, 1989.

The Times, July 9, 1999, p. 1.

U.S. News and World Report. "Economic Theories That Vie For Dominance: Keynesianism, Monetarism—and Now "Supply Side" Ideas; The Course The

Nation Chooses Can Have a Major Impact On Pocketbooks." 92 (April 26, 1982), pp. 55–6.

Walker, Martin. *The President We Deserve, Bill Clinton, His Rise, Falls, and Comebacks*. New York: Crown Publishers, 1996.

Weaver, R. Kent. "The Politics of Blame Avoidance," *Journal of Public Policy*, 6 (1986), pp. 371–96,

Webb, Michael. "International Economic Structures, Government Interests, and International Coordination of Macroeconomic Adjustment Policies," *International Organization*, 45 (1991), pp. 309–42.

Weiner, A.J. and Kahn, H. *Crisis and Arms Control*. Harmon-on-Hudson, NY: Hudson Institute, 1992, cited in David L. Sills, ed. *International Encyclopedia of the Social Sciences*, Vol. 3. New York: Macmillan and the Free Press, 1968.

Weir, Margaret, ed. *The Social Divide: Political Parties and the Future of Activist Government*. Washington, DC: Brookings Institution Press, 1998.

Woodward, Bob. *The Agenda: Inside the Clinton White House*. New York: Simon and Schuster, 1994.

Index

Printed in Great Britain
by Amazon

64580283R00102